JN084838

COMPASS JAPANESE [INTERMEDIATE] INTERACTIVE WORKBOOK

First edition: June 2022

Kurosio Publishers
4-3, Nibancho, Chiyoda-ku, Tokyo 102-0084, Japan
https://www.9640.jp

ISBN 978-4-87424-902-4

Printed in Japan

コンパス日本語 中級

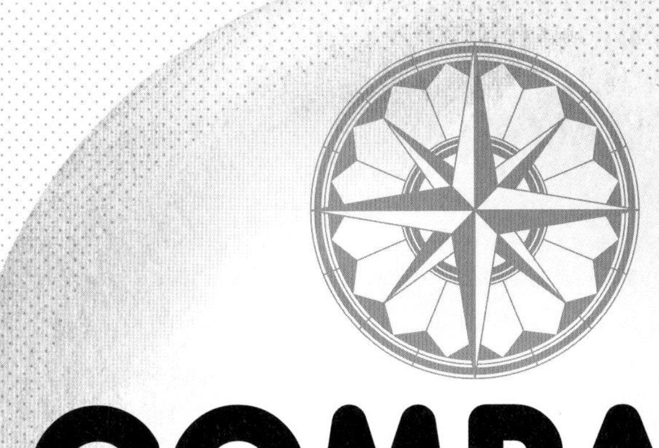

COMPASS JAPANESE

INTERMEDIATE

INTERACTIVE WORKBOOK

Yo Azama 安座間 喜治 | Atsuko Kiuchi 木内 厚子 | Mio Nishimura 西村 美緒 | Michelle Lupisan ミシェル・ルピサン

Kurosio Publishers

Welcome Aboard!

We are excited that you are joining us on a journey - a journey of making the world a better place for all. What can we do for and with our fellow global citizens to improve our mutual quality of life?

We believe such a journey must begin with an understanding of our fellow global citizens. **Compass** provides you with opportunities to explore and discuss universal issues while learning the Japanese language and its cultural perspectives. While **Compass** offers key learning events, you are still the driver of your own journey. Each lesson ends with an action project where you are tasked to make an impact in Japanese whether it's small or big. Imagine yourself completing such important tasks - all in Japanese! You will be so proud, and so will we.

As much as accomplishing the tasks at the end of each lesson feels great, the best part of being on the journey is the experience with your fellow learners and your sensei. **Compass'** activities allow you to experience learning with your partner, small group members, whole class, and sometimes fellow **Compass** users around the world! You will never have to feel alone on this journey. Your greatest resource is your sensei. Remember, they are here to support you. Reach out to them and ask them questions. They want to help you be successful.

As with any journey, traveling in a group can feel daunting and frustrating sometimes. Be patient with yourself and others when you feel overwhelmed. Be patient with your own level, and the levels of others. You are all in this together and we are better together!

Pack your **Compass** and begin your journey with us.

June 2022
Team Compass

My Intentions and Commitment for Learning Japanese

Intention and commitment are key for successful language learning. Take a moment and think about your intention to learn Japanese. Why do you want to learn Japanese? What do you want to accomplish with Japanese?

My name is ___________________

My intentions to learn Japanese are...

____

____

____

After you write down your intention, think about your commitment to achieve your goal. Do you want to spend 15 minutes studying Japanese before you go to bed? Do you want to commit to practicing writing 5 kanjis a day? Do you want to list keywords in your favorite anime and look up the meaning? Every idea is only effective if we stick to it. What are you ready to commit to?

I'm committed to improving my Japanese by...

____

____

____

As the language is best learned in a positive community, your classmates and teacher are great cheerleaders for you. You are expected to be the same for them. Share your intentions and commitment with your classmates and teacher. Have them sign to be your accountability partners. They will check on your progress as you check on their progress periodically.

My accountability partners are...

1.________________________________

2.________________________________

3.________________________________

CONTENTS

COMPASS JAPANESE INTERMEDIATE
INTERACTIVE WORKBOOK WEBSITE

- Sensei's Presentation
- Audio Narration
- ことばリスト（Vocabulary List）
- Task Sheet & Rubrics
- Teacher's Guide

https://www.9640.jp/compass/

Learning Journey Map
- Lesson Organization -

Just like with any journey, knowing the plan is important for one's success. What does your learning journey look like? The Compass Interactive Workbook offers 6 units with urgent and intriguing global themes such as how to live harmoniously with technology, cultural and social identities, and living a purposeful life as a global citizen. Each unit is organized by 2 lessons with focused topics. Each lesson includes 2 short learning cycles to promote language skill building while acquiring new knowledge. A Learning Cycle offers opportunities to reflect and interact with your learning partner, classmates, and communities outside of the classroom!

A sense of accomplishment is key for language learning. Two meaningful tasks (mid task and final task) ensure great opportunities for you to use Japanese to make an impact in the world. Finally, end your lesson by reflecting on your learning. The "Can-do List" at the end of this workbook helps you organize what you have learned as well as what you can now do.

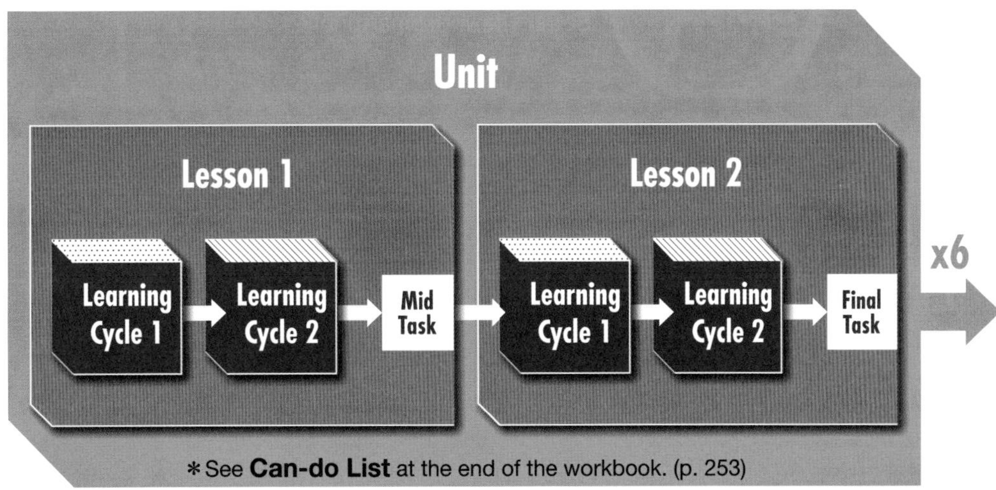

* See **Can-do List** at the end of the workbook. (p. 253)

Before you begin,
First, the lesson begins with essential questions that make you wonder. These questions are essential to activate your curiosity. You and your teacher may modify or add more questions. After all, life without wonder is not exciting. The Can-do List offers what you should be able to do with Japanese at the end of the lesson. Knowing what skills you are developing helps you focus during lesson.

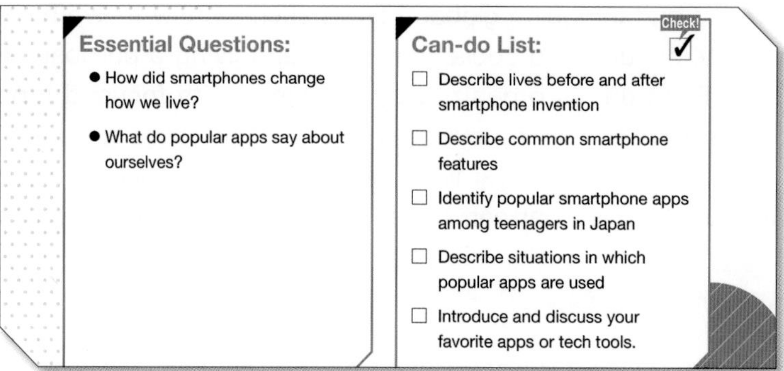

Essential Questions:
● How did smartphones change how we live?
● What do popular apps say about ourselves?
Can-do List:
Check!
☐ Describe lives before and after smartphone invention
☐ Describe common smartphone features
☐ Identify popular smartphone apps among teenagers in Japan
☐ Describe situations in which popular apps are used
☐ Introduce and discuss your favorite apps or tech tools.

The flow of each cycle is described at the beginning to give you an idea of how a lesson progresses.

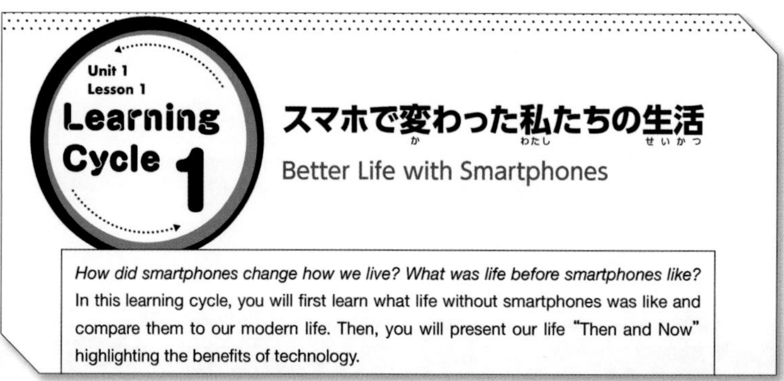

Unit 1
Lesson 1
Learning Cycle 1
スマホで変わった私たちの生活
Better Life with Smartphones
How did smartphones change how we live? What was life before smartphones like?
In this learning cycle, you will first learn what life without smartphones was like and compare them to our modern life. Then, you will present our life "Then and Now" highlighting the benefits of technology.

Learning Cycle

Each learning cycle is organized by the **Global Competence Framework** to guide your learning:

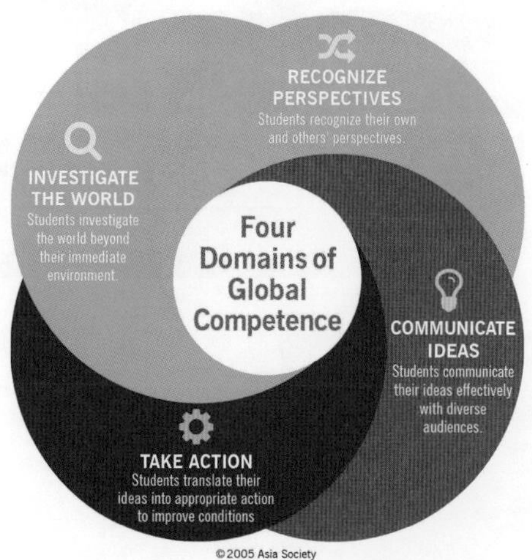

0 考えてみよう Let's Explore!

Before you begin your journey, take a moment to think about what you already know about the topic. What do you notice in the illustration? Use the graphic to organize your thinking and brainstorm what you know or think you know about the topic.

Title picture　　　　Mind map

1 探ってみよう Investigate the World

In this section, your teacher presents the topic and key information about it. Use your current knowledge of the topic to connect with the topic. Pay attention to the teacher's presentation and jot down notes, ask questions, and share your thoughts. Alternatively, you can watch the pre-recorded presentation so you can hear multiple times at your own pace.

Activity 1

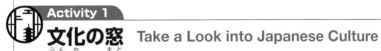

文化の窓 Take a Look into Japanese Culture

Listen to the teacher's presentation and jot down keywords.

PPT Sample presentation is available online.

Activity 2

まとめてみよう Graphic Organizer

Visually organize the information from the teacher's presentation.

2 いろいろな視点(してん)を学(まな)ぼう Recognize Diverse Perspectives

After investigating the topic from the presentation, you will go deeper into perspectives through reading articles, stories, infographics, etc. While some content may resonate with you right away, you may also notice your judgment creeping in as you are learning different perspectives. That's normal. Just stay curious for now as you continue your learning.

Activity 3
読(よ)んで学(まな)ぼう Read and Learn

1 読(よ)んでみよう Let's Read!

Interact with text and answer the questions.
Audio for the reading is also available online.
Download vocabulary list online.

2 Various ways to organize new information are offered here.

- **順番(じゅんばん)に並(なら)べよう Sequencing**
- **ランキング Ranking**
- **分(わ)けてみよう Categorizing**
- **正(ただ)しい？間違(まちが)い？ True and False**
- **マッチング Matching**
- **チェックリスト Checklist**
- **空欄(くうらん)に入(い)れよう Filling in the Blanks/Chart**

Activity 4
ペアでシェアしよう Pair Share

Share your answers from the reading with your partner.

Activity 5
グループでシェアしよう Group Share

Share your ideas in a small group.

Activity 6
質問(しつもん)に答(こた)えよう Respond to the Questions

Based on the reading and group discussion, respond to the questions.

3 アイデアを交換しよう Communicate Ideas

Now that you have analyzed information and reflected on new perspectives, you must have a lot to talk about! This section provides you opportunities to communicate with others about the topic in Japanese. New language structures that help you express your ideas will be highlighted and examined here. In addition to new Japanese language structures, you will also practice how to be a good listener and conversationalist in Japanese.

Activity 7
文法パターンを見つけよう
Let's Explore Language Structure!

1 聞いてみよう Let's Listen!

Observe the teacher's presentation and pay attention to the meaning.

PPT Sample presentation is also available online.

2 新しい文法パターンは？ Where is a New Language Structure?

Examine the provided sentences and look for the pattern(s).

3 意味は？ What Could It Mean?

Discuss the possible meaning and patterns as class.

4 使い方は？ How Can We Use It?

Discuss ways we can use the language patterns in class.

5 使ってみよう Let's Use the New Language Structure!

Use the new language pattern in new situations.

Activity 8
書いてみよう Write It Out

Address your ideas using the new language pattern.

Activity 9
ペアでシェアしよう Pair Share

Share your ideas with your partner.

Activity 10
まとめてみよう Organize Discussion

Organize your thoughts using the new language pattern.

Activity 11

ディスカッションしよう Group Discussion

Discuss with group members about the given topic. Organize discussion using the graphic.

Activity 12

すらすら読(よ)もう Read Fluently

Read the text out loud while focusing on fluency.

Sample audio file is available online.

Activity 13

要約(ようやく)しよう Let's Summarize!

Summarize the reading in your own words.

4 日本語(にほんご)でやってみよう Let's Show What We Can Do!

We can only build confidence by actually doing things ourselves. Don't worry too much about doing things perfectly the first time. Instead, think about it as an opportunity to receive helpful feedback from your teacher and classmates. How can we get better without trying on our own, right?

日本語(にほんご)でアクション！ Take Action in Japanese!

Action speaks louder than words. But action with words speaks even louder! In this final section, you get to accomplish tasks that can make positive impacts in your own community using Japanese. Then, end your learning journey with some self-reflection. What were you the most proud of on your journey? How did you overcome challenges? How did your thinking about the topic change or evolve?

Mid Task

Mid Task is an opportunity for you to try out your Japanese by doing a smaller task.

Final Task

Final Task gives you an opportunity to perform an action that makes an impact in the world.

Task sheet and rubrics can be downloaded online.

We learn from reflecting on our experiences.

Use **Can-do List (p.253)** to reflect and celebrate your accomplishments!

Unit 1 私たちの生活とテクノロジー Technology and Our Lives

How can we better live with our technology?

Lesson 1 スマホで生活向上 Improved Life with Smartphones

Essential Questions:

- How did smartphones change how we live?
- What do popular apps say about ourselves?

Can-do List:

- [ ] Describe lives before and after smartphone invention
- [ ] Describe common smartphone features
- [ ] Identify popular smartphone apps among teenagers in Japan
- [ ] Describe situations in which popular apps are used
- [ ] Introduce and discuss your favorite apps or tech tools.

スマホで変わった私たちの生活

Better Life with Smartphones

How did smartphones change how we live? What was life before smartphones like? In this learning cycle, you will first learn what life without smartphones was like and compare them to our modern life. Then, you will present our life "Then and Now" highlighting the benefits of technology.

0 考えてみよう Let's Explore!

What do you notice in the title picture? (p.13) What ideas come to your mind when you think about the topic? Jot down keywords in Japanese below.

便利なテクノロジー

1 探ってみよう Investigate the World

文化の窓 Take a Look into Japanese Culture

PPT

Listen to Sensei's presentation twice. First, take notes on general ideas in English. When you listen a second time, jot down keywords in Japanese.

スマホで変わった私たちの生活 Better Life with Smartphones

What is this information about?	
Keywords in Japanese	

Activity 2

まとめてみよう Graphic Organizer

Demonstrate your understanding of the previous presentation by organizing your ideas below.

2 いろいろな視点を学ぼう Recognize Diverse Perspectives

読んで学ぼう Read and Learn

1 読んでみよう Let's Read!

Read and annotate the article below. Then, answer the following comprehension questions.

スマホで変わった私たちの生活 Better Life with Smartphones

スマホがなかった時代を想像できますか。iPhoneが2007年に登場して私たちの生活はかなり向上しました。昔できなかったことが、スマホ一つですぐにできるようになりました。特に次の三つの点で私たちの生活は便利になったと言えるでしょう。

1) What are the three areas of improvement the author shared?

1. 場所を選ばずにアクセスできる

以前は、家でテレビやビデオを見ていましたが、今はスマホで、どこででも動画を見ることができるようになりました。また、以前は家の電話や公衆電話でしか話せなかったのが、今ではスマホでどこからでも好きなときに話せるようになりました。

2) What are some examples of improved accessibility?

2. SNSの普及

スマホがなかった時代は、電子メールでコミュニケーションを取っていたので、時間がかかっていました。しかし、今ではSNSの利用で、すぐに相手の様子がわかるようになりました。いつでもどこでも気軽にメッセージや写真が共有できるようになりました。また、SNSを通して世界中で新しい友だちを作ったり、いろいろな情報を交換したりできるようになりました。

3) What are examples of benefits of SNS according to the author?

3. 物のデジタル化

以前は、カメラやビデオで写真や動画を撮ったり、プレーヤーで音楽を聞いたりしていました。しかし、今ではスマホで写真や動画を撮ったり、音楽を聞いたりすることができるようになりました。また、初めての場所に行くとき、以前は紙の地図が必要でしたが、今はスマホの道案内でどこへでも行けるようになりました。スマホだけでいろいろなことができるようになったのです。

4) What is the benefit of digitizing items according to the author?

ことばリスト

□生活 □時代 □想像する □登場する □(生活が)向上する □昔 □選ぶ □以前 □動画
□公衆電話 □普及 □電子メール □(コミュニケーションを)取る □利用 □相手 □様子 □気軽に
□共有する □(～を)通して □情報 □交換する □(写真/動画を)撮る □地図 □道案内

2 チェックリスト Checklist

Check off the keywords that apply to the information presented above.

私たちの生活	スマホの登場前	スマホの登場後
例）家でテレビやビデオを見ていた。	✓	
1) どこからでも好きなときに話せるようになった。		
2) SNSの利用で、すぐに相手の様子がわかるようになった。		
3) 紙の地図が必要だった。		
4) 家の電話や公衆電話で話した。		
5) どこででも動画を見ることができるようになった。		
6) 電子メールでコミュニケーションを取った。		
7) スマホの道案内でどこへでも行けるようになった。		

Activity 4 ペアでシェアしよう Pair Share

Share your understanding from the previous activities with your partner.

例）スマホの登場前は、家でテレビやビデオを見ていました。でも、スマホの登場後は、どこででも動画を見ることができるようになりました。

Activity 5 グループでシェアしよう Group Share

Converse with your group members about the topic in Japanese.

例）スマホの登場前は、家でテレビやビデオを見ていました。でも、スマホの登場後は、どこででも動画を見ることができるようになりました。

Activity 6
質問(しつもん)に答(こた)えよう Respond to the Questions

Answer the following questions based on what you have read about the topic.

スマホの登場(とうじょう)で、どんなことができるようになりましたか。

例(れい)) どこからでも、好(す)きなときに話(はな)せるようになりました。

1) ......

2) ......

3) ......

3 アイデアを交換しよう Communicate Ideas

Activity 7
文法(ぶんぽう)パターンを見(み)つけよう Let's Explore Language Structure!

1 聞(き)いてみよう Let's Listen!

PPT

Listen to Sensei's presentation and jot down key ideas.

2 新(あたら)しい文法(ぶんぽう)パターンは？ Where is a New Language Structure?

What is the common language structure? Highlight below.

- 昔(むかし)できなかったことが、スマホ一(ひと)つですぐにできるようになりました。
- どこででも動画(どうが)を見(み)ることができるようになりました。
- すぐに相手(あいて)の様子(ようす)がわかるようになりました。

3 意味(いみ)は？ What Could It Mean?

Discuss possible meanings of the language structure as a class.

4 使い方は？ How Can We Use It?

Discuss possible ways to use the language structure as a class.

5 使ってみよう Let's Use the New Language Structure!

Use the language structure in new situations.

例）インターネットで、何ができるようになりましたか。
いろいろな情報が探せるようになりました。

1）テクノロジーの進歩*で、何ができるようになりましたか。

2）日本語を使って、何ができるようになりましたか。

3）医療技術の進歩*で、何ができるようになりましたか。

* テクノロジーの進歩 development of technology、医療技術の進歩 development of medical technology

書いてみよう Write It Out

Express your ideas in writing using the new language structure.

私の意見：スマホの登場で便利になったこと

1.
2.
3.

Activity 9
ペアでシェアしよう　Pair Share

Share your ideas with your partner using the writings from the previous activity.

例）A: スマホの登場で、便利になったことを教えてください。
B: どこででも動画が見られるようになりました。

__________さんの意見：スマホの登場で便利になったこと

1.
2.
3.

Activity 10
まとめてみよう　Organize Discussion

Organize your discussion with your partner in Japanese.

Activity 11 ディスカッションしよう Group Discussion

Discuss the topic in groups in Japanese. Use the graphic organizer to capture members' ideas, opinions, and feelings. As you listen to members' ideas, jot down key information in the graphic organizer. Finally, write down the commonalities in the middle section.

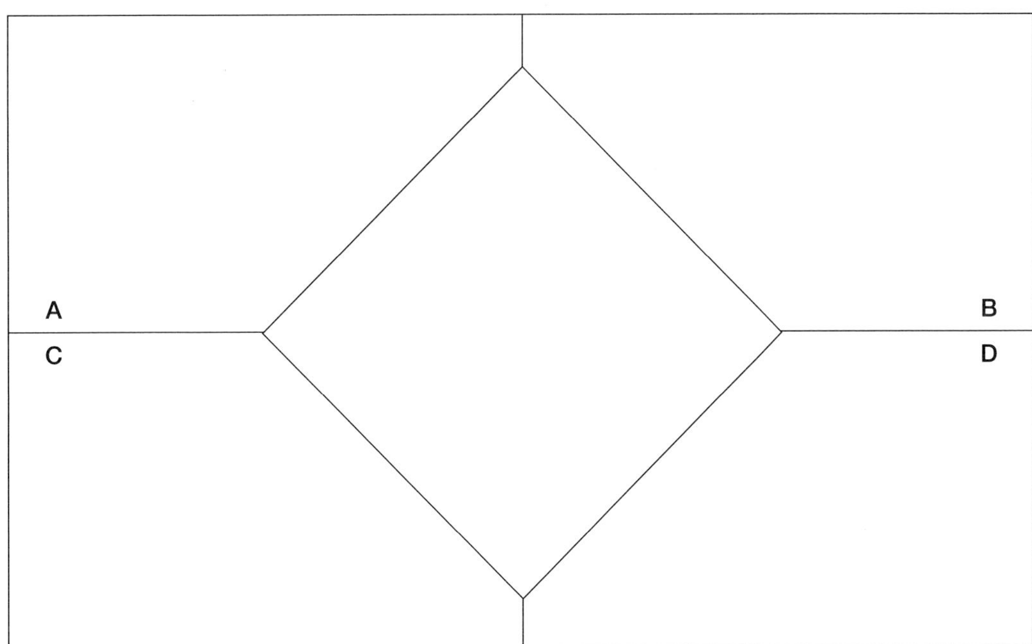

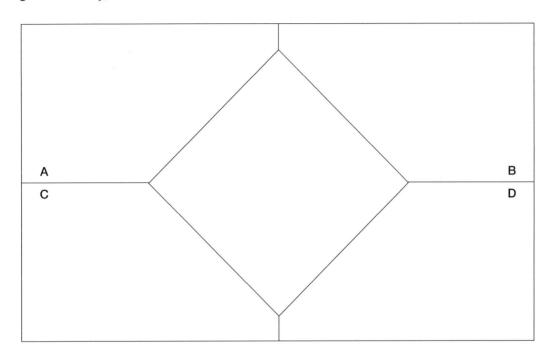

Activity 12 すらすら読もう Read Fluently

Read the article (Activity 3) to your partner. Pay attention to pronunciation, intonation, and tempo as you read aloud.

Activity 13 要約しよう Let's Summarize!

Summarize the article(s) in Japanese.

4 日本語でやってみよう Let's Show What We Can Do!

私たちの生活：昔と今 Our Life: Then and Now (Essay)

In this cycle, you learned about the benefits of smartphones in modern life. Write an essay in which you compare our life before and after the invention of smartphones in order to present this essay at an essay contest in Japan. Highlight how our life was changed and give your opinions about it.

Required

- □ ～ようになりました。
- □ ～に比べて、～
- □ ～と思います。
- □ なぜなら／その理由は、～からです。

Optional

- □ ～ほうが、～
- □ 私の意見としては、～

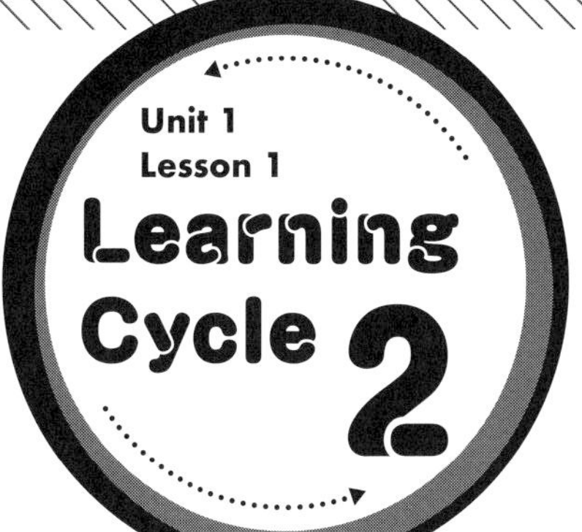

日本の若者に人気のアプリ

Popular Apps Among Young Japanese People

What are popular apps among young Japanese people? In this learning cycle, you will first learn about popular apps in Japan and when they are used. Then, you will ask your classmates about the popular apps. Finally, you will write a report comparing popular apps among Japanese young people and your classmates.

0 考えてみよう Let's Explore!

1 What ideas come to your mind when you think about the topic? Jot down keywords in Japanese below.

人気のアプリ

2 What kind of apps do you use the most? List them based on the genres below.

ゲーム	動画・写真	ショッピング	SNS
	例）Instagram		

1 探ってみよう Investigate the World

Activity 1 文化の窓 Take a Look into Japanese Culture

Listen to Sensei's presentation twice. First, take notes on general ideas in English. When you listen a second time, jot down keywords in Japanese.

日本の若者に人気のアプリ Popular Apps Among Young Japanese People

What is this information about?	
Keywords in Japanese	

Activity 2 まとめてみよう Graphic Organizer

Demonstrate your understanding of the previous presentation by organizing your ideas below.

2 いろいろな視点を学ぼう Recognize Diverse Perspectives

Activity 3 読んで学ぼう Read and Learn

1 読んでみよう Let's Read!

Read and annotate the article below. Then, answer the following comprehension questions.

日本の若者に人気のアプリ

Popular Apps Among Young Japanese People

LINE

日本で一番多く使われているSNSで、二人に一人が利用しています。家族や友だちに連絡するときに、簡単にメッセージを送ったりビデオ通話をしたりすることができます。サービスは無料ですが、有料のスタンプや絵文字を使って、かわいいメッセージを送ることもできます。そして、グループを作って、写真や動画を共有したり、アルバムを作って保存したりすることもできます。さらに、ニュースや情報を受け取ることもできて、いろいろなゲームもあるので、人気があります。

B612

世界中の人が利用している「自撮り専用」のカメラアプリです。自分の写真や動画をかわいく撮りたいときに、便利です。写真や動画をフィルターで好きに加工したり、写真にメッセージを組み合わせて動画にしたりすることもできます。コミュニケーションが取れるカメラアプリとして、注目を集めています。

WEAR

ファッション好きの人たちが利用しているファッションコーディネートアプリです。いろいろなキーワードから、自分が好きなコーディネートを探すことができます。注目のファッションをチェックしたり、興味のあるブランドについて調べたりすることもできます。ファッションのコーディネートに悩んだときに、役立ちます。気に入ったものはファッション通販サイトで買うことができます。

LINE

1) What can you do with this app?

2) Why is this app popular?

B612

1) Who uses this app?

2) What can you do with this app?

WEAR

1) Who uses this app?

2) What can you do with this app?

ことばリスト 

☐若者　☐利用する　☐連絡する　☐(メッセージを)送る　☐ビデオ通話(をする)　☐無料　☐有料

☐絵文字　☐保存する　☐受け取る　☐人気(がある)　☐自撮り　☐専用　☐加工する　☐組み合わせる

☐注目(を集める)　☐探す　☐興味(のある)　☐調べる　☐悩む　☐役立つ　☐気に入る　☐通販

2 分けてみよう Categorizing

Write the keywords in the appropriate categories.

LINE	B612	WEAR
B		

A. 自分の写真や動画をかわいく撮りたいときに使う。
B. 写真や動画を共有したいときに使う。
C. 注目のファッションをチェックしたいときに使う。
D. ビデオ通話をしたいときに使う。
E. 写真や動画を加工したいときに使う。
F. 興味のあるブランドについて調べたいときに使う。
G. ゲームをしたいときに使う。
H. 自分が好きなコーディネートを探したいときに使う。

Activity 4
ペアでシェアしよう Pair Share

Share your understanding from the previous activities with your partner.

例）家族や友だちに連絡するときに、LINE を使います。

Activity 5
グループでシェアしよう Group Share

Converse with your group members about the topic in Japanese.

例）家族や友だちに連絡するときに、LINE を使います。

Activity 6

質問に答えよう Respond to the Questions

Answer the following questions based on what you have read about the topic.

例) どんなときに、LINE を使いますか。

家族や友だちに連絡するときに、使います。

1) どんなときに、B612 を使いますか。

2) どんなときに、WEAR を使いますか。

3) どんなときに、＿＿＿＿＿を使いますか。

3 アイデアを交換しよう Communicate Ideas

Activity 7

文法パターンを見つけよう Let's Explore Language Structure!

1 聞いてみよう Let's Listen!

PPT

Listen to Sensei's presentation and jot down key ideas.

2 新しい文法パターンは？ Where is a New Language Structure?

What is the common language structure? Highlight below.

- B612 は、自分の写真や動画をかわいく撮りたいときに、便利です。
- WEAR は、ファッションのコーディネートに悩んだときに、役立ちます。
- LINE は、家族や友だちに連絡するときに、簡単にメッセージを送ったりビデオ通話をしたりすることができます。

3 意味は？ What Could It Mean?

Discuss possible meanings of the language structure as a class.

4 使い方は？ How Can We Use It?

Discuss possible ways to use the language structure as a class.

5 使ってみよう Let's Use the New Language Structure!

Use the language structure in new situations.

テクノロジー・ツール	どんなときに使う？
例）スマホ	写真や動画をかわいく撮りたいときに、使います。
1）ラップトップパソコン	
2）________	

Activity 8 書いてみよう Write It Out

Express your ideas in writing using the new language structure.

私がよく使うアプリ トップ3

アプリ	どんなときに使う？
1.	
2.	
3.	

Activity 9

ペアでシェアしよう　Pair Share

Share your ideas with your partner using the writings from the previous activity.

例(れい)) A: よく使(つか)うアプリは何(なん)ですか。そのアプリは、どんなときに使(つか)いますか。
B: インスタグラムです。写真(しゃしん)を共有(きょうゆう)したいときに使(つか)います。

＿＿＿＿＿さんがよく使(つか)うアプリ　トップ3

アプリ	どんなときに使(つか)う？
1.	
2.	
3.	

Activity 10

まとめてみよう　Organize Discussion

Organize your discussion with your partner in Japanese.

Activity 11 ディスカッションしよう Group Discussion

Discuss the topic in groups in Japanese. Use the graphic organizer to capture members' ideas, opinions, and feelings. As you listen to members' ideas, jot down key information in the graphic organizer. Finally, write down the commonalities in the middle section.

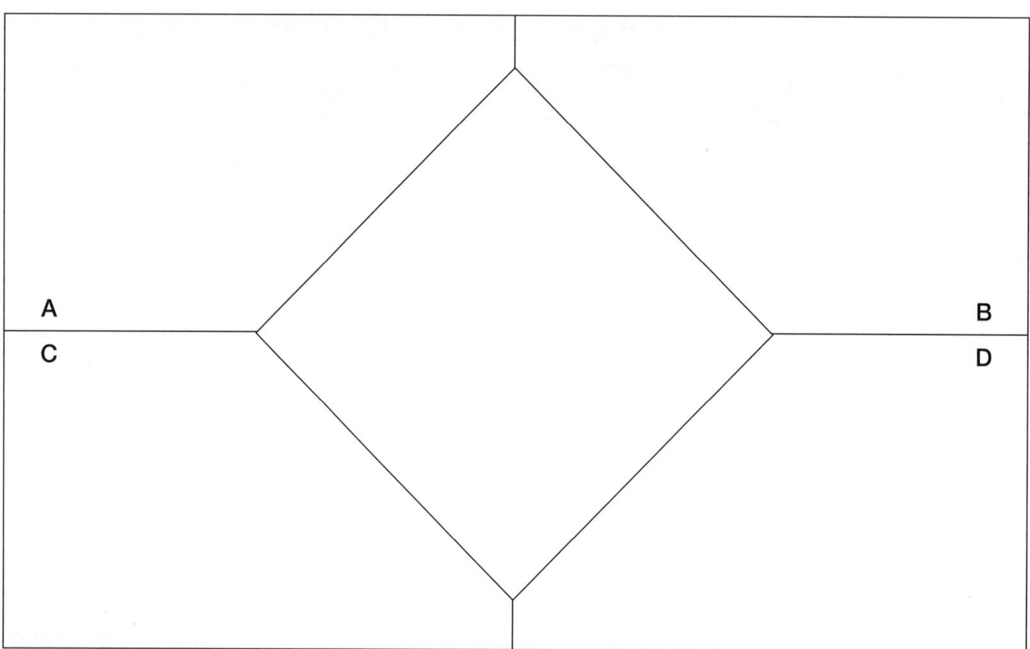

Activity 12 すらすら読(よ)もう Read Fluently

Read the article (Activity 3) to your partner. Pay attention to pronunciation, intonation, and tempo as you read aloud.

Activity 13 要約(ようやく)しよう Let's Summarize!

Summarize the article(s) in Japanese.

4 日本語でやってみよう Let's Show What We Can Do!

人気(にんき)のアプリ Popular Apps (Comparative Report)

You have learned about the most popular apps in Japan and shared with your classmates about apps you use often. Write a report comparing popular apps among Japanese young people and your classmates in order to upload your report to a Japanese blog. Introduce the most popular apps and give descriptions of each.

Required

- □ ～ときに、～
- □ ～に比(くら)べて、～
- □ ～と思(おも)います。
- □ なぜなら／その理由(りゆう)は、～からです。

Optional

- □ ～ほうが、～
- □ 一方(いっぽう)で、～
- □ 私(わたし)の意見(いけん)としては、～

Unit 1 Mid Task

日本語でアクション！

Take Action in Japanese!

You are making a video message for high schoolers in Japan who want to learn about smarthphone apps or tech tools in your countries.

Choice 1: 私のスマホの中身紹介

Apps on My Smartphone (Video)

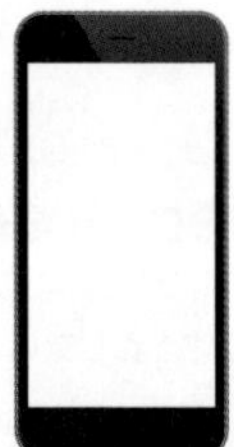

Introduce your favorite and most used apps to Japanese high schoolers by making your own "What's on My Smartphone" video. Describe your recommended apps, giving reasons why you like them, and when you would use them.

アプリ	説明

Choice 2: 私の好きなテクノロジー・ツール

My Favorite Technology Tools (Video)

Introduce your favorite technology tools to Japanese high schoolers by making an introduction video. Describe your recommended tech tool(s), giving reasons why you like them, how they improved your life, and when you would use them.

テクノロジー・ツール	説明

Unit 1 私たちの生活とテクノロジー
Technology and Our Lives

How can we better live with our technology?

Lesson 2 スマホと私
Smartphone and I

Essential Questions:

- What are the negative effects of using a smartphone?
- How does smartphone use affect our lives?
- How can we live better with smartphones?

Can-do List:

- ☐ Identify issues surrounding smartphone addiction
- ☐ Find out and describe issues students may be experiencing
- ☐ Suggest some solutions that help to cope with smartphone usage
- ☐ Present issues surrounding smartphone usage and the effects on self/other and results

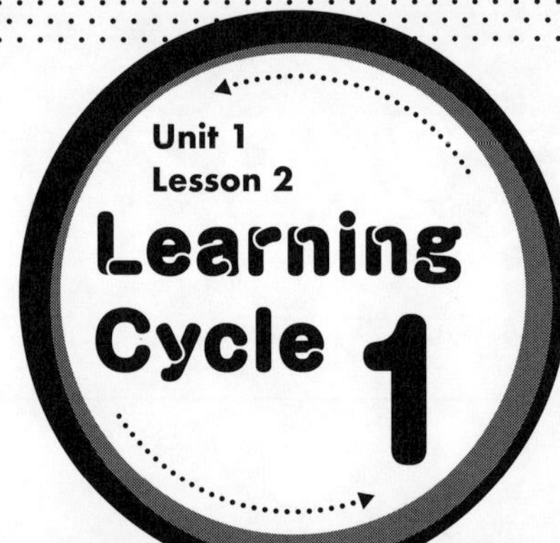

スマホの悪影響（あくえいきょう）

Negative Effects of Smartphones

What are the negative effects of smartphones? How is smartphone use affecting our lives? In this learning cycle, you will first learn about the possible effects of using smartphones. Then, you will discuss the benefits and negative effects of smartphones with classmates. Finally, you will write an argumentative essay for Japanese online news addressing such effects.

0 考えてみよう Let's Explore!

What do you notice in the title picture? (p.33) What ideas come to your mind when you think about the topic? Jot down keywords in Japanese below.

スマホの悪影響（あくえいきょう）

1 探ってみよう Investigate the World

Activity 1 文化の窓 Take a Look into Japanese Culture

PPT

Listen to Sensei's presentation twice. First, take notes on general ideas in English. When you listen a second time, jot down keywords in Japanese.

スマホの悪影響 Negative Effects of Smartphones

What is this information about?	
Keywords in Japanese	

Activity 2 まとめてみよう Graphic Organizer

Demonstrate your understanding of the previous presentation by organizing your ideas below.

2 いろいろな視点を学ぼう Recognize Diverse Perspectives

Activity 3 読んで学ぼう Read and Learn

1 読んでみよう Let's Read!

Read and annotate the article below. Then, answer the following comprehension questions.

スマホの悪影響 Negative Effects of Smartphones

先生：スマホには、利点も難点もありますね。例えば、家族や友だちとすぐに連絡がとれることは利点ですが、一方で、「スマホ依存症」になるという難点もあります。いつもスマホをチェックする、スマホを持っていないと落ち着かない、スマホの利用がやめられないことを「スマホ依存症」と言います。スマホを使いすぎたら、体に悪い影響を与えますよね。どんな影響を与えると思いますか。

生徒 A：スマホで動画や SNS などを見すぎたら、目に悪い影響を与えると思います。

先生：そうですね。目が疲れたり、ドライアイになったりしますね。利用時間をコントロールしないと、視力も落ちるでしょう。ほかに意見がありますか。

生徒 B：スマホを使いすぎたら、脳にも悪い影響を与えると思います。

先生：たしかに。スマホは便利すぎて、自分で考えて行動する必要がなくなりますね。その結果、脳を使う機会が少なくなって、思考力が落ちるかもしれません。ほかにはどうですか。

生徒 C：夜遅くまでスマホでゲームをしたり、動画や SNS を見たりしていたら、睡眠時間が減ると思います。

先生：そうですね。脳が興奮して、眠れなくなることがありますね。その結果、睡眠不足になってしまいます。寝る前にスマホをオフにするなど、どうしたら、スマホを使いすぎないか、みんなで考えてみましょう。

1) Based on this dialogue, what are some of the negative side effects of excessive use of smartphones?

2) What does the teacher suggest students do to avoid lack of sleep/insomnia?

ことばリスト

□悪影響　□利点　□難点　□依存症　□落ち着く　□～すぎる　□影響　□(影響を)与える　□視力
あくえいきょう　りてん　なんてん　いぞんしょう　お　つ　　　　えいきょう　えいきょう　あた　しりょく

□(視力／思考力が)落ちる　□脳　□行動する　□必要がない　□結果　□機会　□思考力　□睡眠時間
しりょく　しこうりょく　お　　のう　こうどう　　ひつよう　　けっか　きかい　しこうりょく　すいみんじかん

□減る　□興奮する　□睡眠不足
へ　　こうふん　　すいみんぶそく

2 正しい？間違い？ True and False

Read the statements. Write true (○) or false (×) accordingly.

例) スマホを使いすぎたら、自分で考えて行動するようになる。	×
1) スマホを使いすぎたら、睡眠不足になる。	
2) スマホを使いすぎたら、目がよくなる。	
3) スマホを使いすぎたら、脳を使う機会が増える。	
4) スマホを使いすぎたら、視力が落ちる。	
5) スマホを使いすぎたら、思考力が落ちる。	

Activity 4 ペアでシェアしよう Pair Share

Share your understanding from the previous activities with your partner.

例) スマホを使いすぎたら、視力が落ちます。

Activity 5 グループでシェアしよう Group Share

Converse with your group members about the topic in Japanese.

例) スマホを使いすぎたら、視力が落ちます。

Activity 6
質問に答えよう Respond to the Questions

Answer the following questions based on what you have read about the topic.

例）何をしすぎたら、目に悪い影響を与えますか。

動画を見すぎたら、視力が落ちます。

1) 何をしすぎたら、思考力が落ちますか。

2) 何をしすぎたら、睡眠時間が減りますか。

3) 何をしすぎたら、脳に悪い影響を与えますか。

3 アイデアを交換しよう Communicate Ideas

Activity 7
文法パターンを見つけよう Let's Explore Language Structure!

1 聞いてみよう Let's Listen!

PPT

Listen to Sensei's presentation and jot down key ideas.

2 新しい文法パターンは？ Where is a New Language Structure?

What is the common language structure? Highlight below.

- スマホを使いすぎたら、体に悪い影響を与えます。
- スマホで動画やSNSなどを見すぎたら、目に悪い影響を与えると思います。
- スマホを使いすぎたら、脳にも悪い影響を与えると思います。

3 意味は？ What Could It Mean?

Discuss possible meanings of the language structure as a class.

4 使い方は？ How Can We Use It?

Discuss possible ways to use the language structure as a class.

5 使ってみよう Let's Use the New Language Structure!

Use the language structure in new situations.

例）何をしすぎたら、視力が落ちますか。
動画を見すぎたら、視力が落ちます。

1） 何をしすぎたら、眠れなくなりますか。

2） 何をしすぎたら、体に悪いですか。

3） どんなことを考えすぎたら、心配になりますか。

Activity 8 書いてみよう Write It Out

Express your ideas in writing using the new language structure.

私の意見：スマホの利点と難点

利点	難点
•	•
•	•

Activity 9
ペアでシェアしよう　Pair Share

Share your ideas with your partner using the writings from the previous activity.

例）A: スマホの利点と難点を教えてください。

B: 利点は、家族や友だちとすぐに連絡が取れることです。難点は、使いすぎたら、視力が落ちることです。

＿＿＿＿＿＿さんの意見：スマホの利点と難点

利点	難点
•	•
•	•

Activity 10
まとめてみよう　Organize Discussion

Organize your discussion with your partner in Japanese.

Activity 11 ディスカッションしよう Group Discussion

Discuss the topic in groups in Japanese. Use the graphic organizer to capture members' ideas, opinions, and feelings. As you listen to members' ideas, jot down key information in the graphic organizer. Finally, write down the commonalities in the middle section.

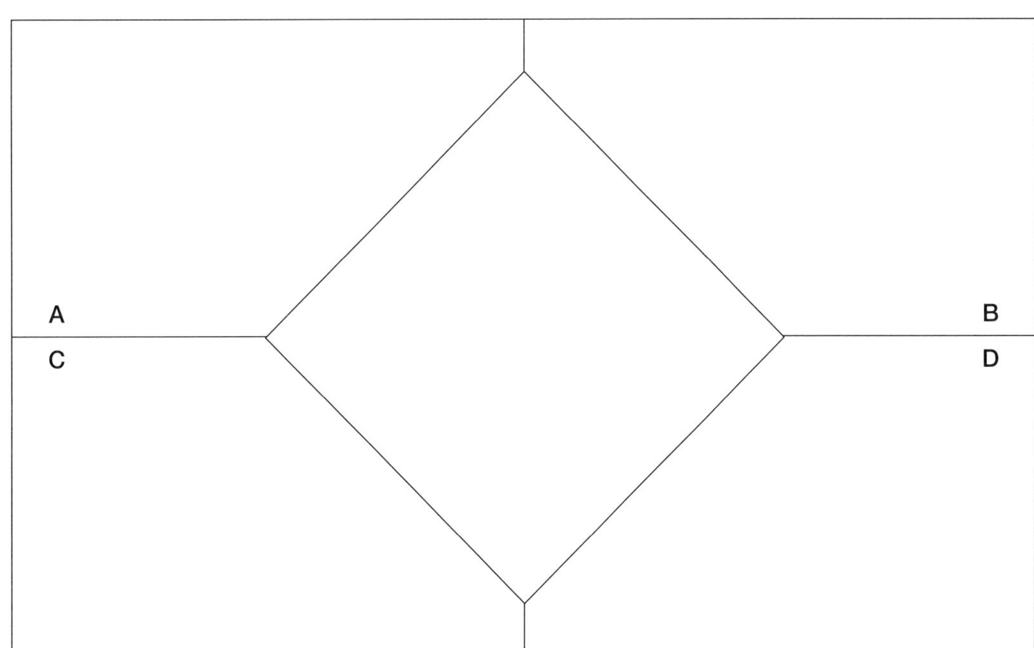

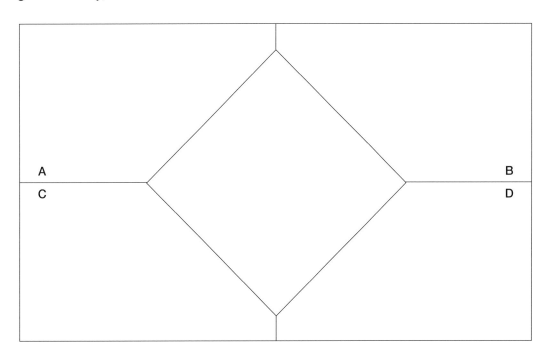

Activity 12 すらすら読もう Read Fluently

Read the article (Activity 3) to your partner. Pay attention to pronunciation, intonation, and tempo as you read aloud.

Activity 13 要約しよう Let's Summarize!

Summarize the article(s) in Japanese.

日本語でやってみよう Let's Show What We Can Do!

スマホ依存症(いぞんしょう)について

On Smartphone Addiction (Argumentative Essay)

You are invited to be a writer for a school online newspaper in Japan, which is focusing on "smartphone addiction." Write an argumentative essay on the influence of smartphone usage. To strengthen your argument, address the opposing side by stating the pros of smartphones, then transition into the negative effects of smartphones. Lastly, state your opinion on the effects of smartphone addiction, and reflect on why it is important to limit our smartphone use.

NEWS

Main Issue(s):

Pros:

Cons:

Personal Opinions:

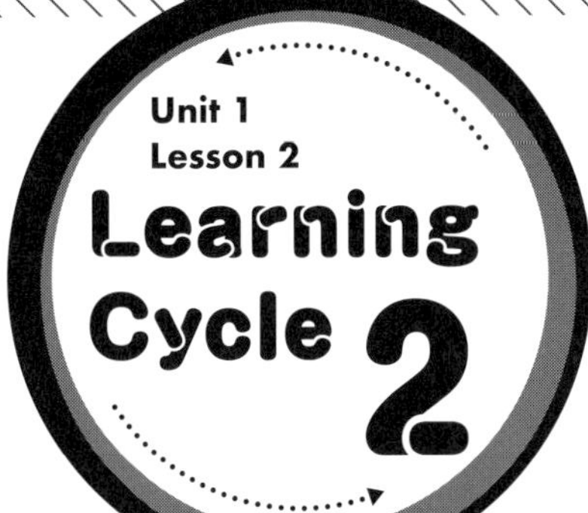

スマホとの賢い付き合い方

How to Live with Our Smartphones

How can we live better with smartphones? In this learning cycle, you will first learn about some ways to overcome smartphone addiction. Then, you will exchange possible solutions with classmates. Finally, you will respond to an online community forum with suggestions.

0 考えてみよう Let's Explore!

What ideas come to your mind when you think about the topic? Jot down keywords in Japanese below.

スマホと私

1 探ってみよう Investigate the World

Activity 1 文化の窓 Take a Look into Japanese Culture

Listen to Sensei's presentation twice. First, take notes on general ideas in English. When you listen a second time, jot down keywords in Japanese.

スマホとの賢い付き合い方 How to Live with Our Smartphones

What is this information about?	
Keywords in Japanese	

Activity 2 まとめてみよう Graphic Organizer

Demonstrate your understanding of the previous presentation by organizing your ideas below.

2 いろいろな視点を学ぼう Recognize Diverse Perspectives

Activity 3 読んで学ぼう Read and Learn

1 読んでみよう Let's Read!

Read and annotate the article below. Then, answer the following comprehension questions.

スマホとの賢い付き合い方 How to Live with Our Smartphones

04

スマホ依存症を治したいのですが、
どうしたらいいですか。

1．通知をオフにする

通知が来たとき、スマホが気になってしまいます。仕事や勉強に集中できないので、スマホの通知を止めてサウンドをオフにするといいですよ。

2．使用時間を決める

スマホを使う時間と使わない時間を決めるといいです。例えば、「食事のときや勉強のときはスマホを使わない」など、ルールを決めるといいですよ。

3．目覚まし時計を使う

朝、起きるためにスマホのアラームを使う人が多いですが、そうすると寝る前にスマホを見てしまいます。無理だと思っても、スマホは寝室に持って行かないほうがいいです。スマホの代わりに、目覚まし時計を使うといいですよ。試してみてください。

What are the three suggested strategies to avoid smartphone addiction?

1.

2.

3.

ことばリスト

□賢い　□付き合い方　□(依存症を)治す　□通知　□気になる　□集中する　□(通知を)止める
□使用時間　□決める　□目覚まし時計　□無理　□寝室　□持って行く　□代わりに　□試す

2 チェックリスト Checklist

Check off the keywords that apply to the information presented above.

スマホ依存症の治し方	私はできる	私は無理
1) 通知をオフにするといい。		
2) スマホを使わない時間を決めるといい。		
3) 目覚まし時計を使うといい。		
4) 寝る前にスマホを見ないほうがいい。		
5) スマホを寝室に持って行かないほうがいい。		

Activity 4
ペアでシェアしよう Pair Share

Share your understanding from the previous activities with your partner.

例）スマホ依存症を治すためには、通知をオフにするといいと思います。でも、私は無理です。

Activity 5
グループでシェアしよう Group Share

Converse with your group members about the topic in Japanese.

例）スマホ依存症を治すためには、通知をオフにするといいと思います。でも、私は無理です。

Activity 6
質問に答えよう Respond to the Questions

Answer the following questions based on what you have read about the topic.

例）スマホの使いすぎで目が痛いんですが、どうしたらいいですか。
スマホを使う時間を決めるといいですよ。

1）スマホが気になって勉強に集中できないんですが、どうしたらいいですか。

2）寝る前にスマホを見てしまうんですが、どうしたらいいですか。

3）スマホのゲームのしすぎで睡眠不足なんですが、どうしたらいいですか。

4）スマホを持っていないと落ち着かないんですが、どうしたらいいですか。

3 アイデアを交換しよう Communicate Ideas

Activity 7
文法パターンを見つけよう Let's Explore Language Structure!

1 聞いてみよう Let's Listen!

Listen to Sensei's presentation and jot down key ideas.

2 新しい文法パターンは？ Where is a New Language Structure?

What is the common language structure? Highlight below.

- スマホの通知を止めてサウンドをオフにするといいです。
- スマホを使う時間と使わない時間を決めるといいです。
- スマホの代わりに、目覚まし時計を使うといいです。

3 意味は？ What Could It Mean?

Discuss possible meanings of the language structure as a class.

4 使い方は？ How Can We Use It?

Discuss possible ways to use the language structure as a class.

5 使ってみよう Let's Use the New Language Structure!

Use the language structure in new situations.

問題	対策
例）スマホの通知が気になります。	通知をオフにするといいです。
1）勉強に集中できません。	
2）スマホでゲームをしすぎてしまいます。	
3）体力がありません。	
4）＿＿＿＿＿＿＿＿	

Activity 8
書いてみよう Write It Out

Express your ideas in writing using the new language structure.

私の意見：スマホとの賢い付き合い方

1.
2.
3.

Activity 9 ペアでシェアしよう Pair Share

Share your ideas with your partner using the writings from the previous activity.

____________さんの意見（いけん）：スマホとの賢（かしこ）い付（つ）き合（あ）い方（かた）

例（れい）) A: スマホを使（つか）いすぎて困（こま）っているんですが、どうしたらいいですか。

B: スマホの通知（つうち）をオフにするといいですよ。

1.
2.
3.

Activity 10 まとめてみよう Organize Discussion

Organize your discussion with your partner in Japanese.

Activity 11
ディスカッションしよう Group Discussion

Discuss the topic in groups in Japanese. Use the graphic organizer to capture members' ideas, opinions, and feelings. As you listen to members' ideas, jot down key information in the graphic organizer. Finally, write down the commonalities in the middle section.

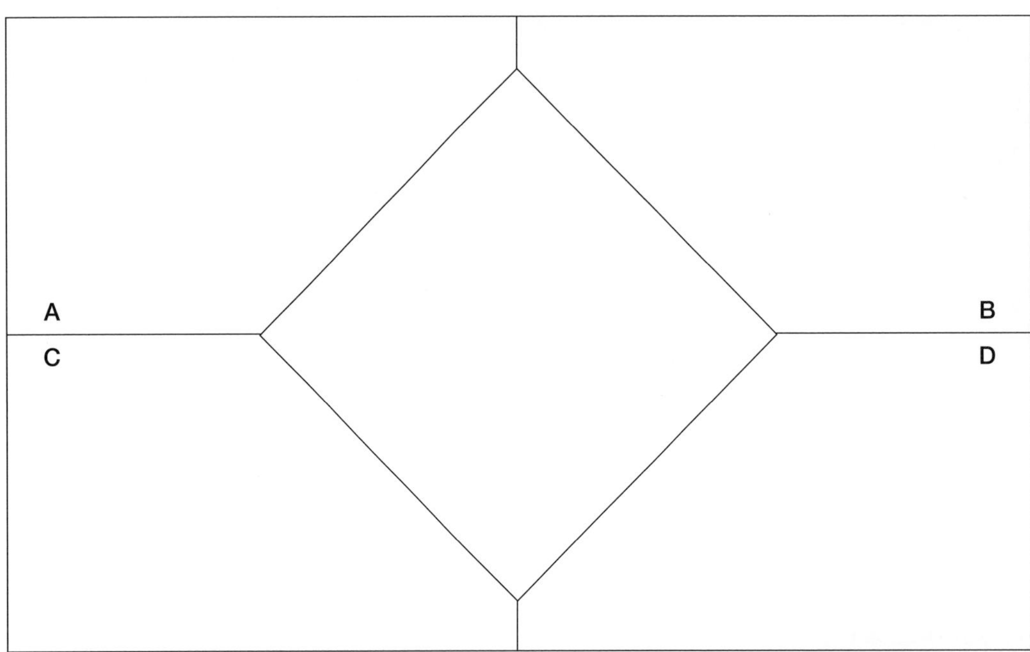

Activity 12
すらすら読もう Read Fluently

Read the article (Activity 3) to your partner. Pay attention to pronunciation, intonation, and tempo as you read aloud.

Activity 13
要約しよう Let's Summarize!

Summarize the article(s) in Japanese.

4 日本語でやってみよう Let's Show What We Can Do!

スマホ依存症の悩み相談

Smartphone Addiction (Online Community Forum)

You have just viewed messages on an online community forum from students in Japan suffering from smartphone addiction. Write a response to one of the messages from the forum. Be sure to include the following points in your response:

- Briefly restate or paraphrase the issue. In this way, the person feels s/he was heard.
- Relate to the person as you share your similar experience from past or present.
- Provide suggestions.

Read the following sample and identify the above elements.

Sample:

けんじさん、メッセージを読みました。スマホのせいで睡眠時間が減って困っているんですね。私も以前、同じ経験がありました。友だちからのメッセージが多くて、スマホの通知が気になって、眠れませんでした。スマホを使いすぎたら、体に悪い影響がたくさんあるそうです。対策として、寝る前にスマホをオフにするといいですよ。試してみてください。

Unit 1 Final Task

日本語でアクション！

Take Action in Japanese!

上を向いて歩こう Look Up!

Task Sheet & Rubrics 

How can we better live with our smartphones? How much time do you spend looking at your phone? Here's an opportunity to raise your awareness of the dangers of smartphone addiction among teens in Japan. Your task is to promote healthy relationships with our smartphones.

Your Role & Purpose	PSA producer to raise awareness of the danger of smartphone addiction among Japanese teens.
Your Audience	Japanese high school students
Language	☐ Provide attention-catching introduction ☐ Describe negative effects of smartphone addiction ☐ Report hearsay with evidence ☐ Suggestions
Product	**Product Type:** ☐ PSA video (slideshow, commercial, etc.) 2-5 minutes **Optional:** ☐ Brochure or flyer

Unit 2 進化するデザイン Evolving Design

しんか

How does design impact our everyday lives?

Lesson 1 日本の製品とデザイン Japanese Products and Design

にほん　せいひん

Essential Questions:

- What is Japanese design?
- How do design and function relate to each other?
- How does culture influence design?
- What does it take to make an attractive product?

Can-do List:

- ☐ Identify key elements of Japanese design
- ☐ Discuss important criteria when purchasing products
- ☐ Review a product of my choice
- ☐ Compare your country's and Japanese products

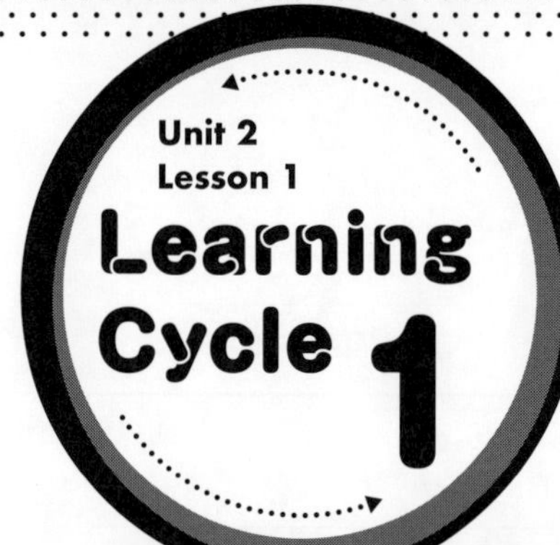

日本の製品：機能と特徴

Japanese Products: Functions and Characteristics

What is Japanese design? How do design and function relate to each other? In this learning cycle, you will first learn about the functions and characteristics of Japanese products. Then, you will survey your classmates to brainstorm important features when choosing a product. Finally, you will choose the top one Japanese product that you wish to use and describe its functions and characteristics.

0 考えてみよう Let's Explore!

What do you notice in the title picture? (p.53) What ideas come to your mind when you think about the topic? Jot down keywords in Japanese below.

日本の製品

1 探ってみよう Investigate the World

Activity 1 文化の窓 Take a Look into Japanese Culture

Listen to Sensei's presentation twice. First, take notes on general ideas in English. When you listen a second time, jot down keywords in Japanese.

日本の製品：機能と特徴 Japanese Products: Functions and Characteristics

ペン型はさみ	
魚焼きグリル	
温水洗浄便座	

Activity 2 まとめてみよう Graphic Organizer

Demonstrate your understanding of the previous presentation by organizing your ideas below.

2 いろいろな視点を学ぼう Recognize Diverse Perspectives

Activity 3 読んで学ぼう Read and Learn

1 読んでみよう Let's Read!

Read and annotate the article below. Then, answer the following comprehension questions.

日本の製品：機能と特徴

Japanese Products: Functions and Characteristics

日本の製品は、デザインも機能も優れていることで、世界で知られています。例えば、文房具、台所用品、そして生活用品など、ユニークな機能と特徴があります。これから、その中のいくつかを紹介します。

1. 消せるペン

消せるペンには、温度で色が変わるフリクションインクが使われています。えんぴつと同じように消せるので、何度でも書いたり消したりしたいときに便利です。ボールペンや蛍光ペンなど種類もいろいろあります。でも、高温になると、インクが消えてしまうので、注意が必要です。

2. 圧力 IH 炊飯器

炊飯器は、ご飯を炊くときに使います。現在は、高温で炊く圧力 IH の炊飯器が人気があります。お米がふっくらとおいしく炊けるからです。炊飯器にはいろいろな機能があります。保温中に自動でスチームが入る「スチーム保温」機能や、お米によって炊き方が変えられる「炊き分け」機能などもあります。そのほか、パンやケーキ、シチューやカレーなどが作れる「調理コース」機能も付いていて、とても便利です。

3. こたつ

こたつは、寒い冬に足や体を温めたいときに使います。テーブルの下にヒーターが付いていて、こたつのふとんをかけます。温度が調節できるので、とても便利です。テーブルの形が丸や四角など、デザインや形もいろいろあります。一度こたつに入ったら気持ちがよくて出られなくなるので、気をつけましょう。

What are some unique features of the following products?

1) Item 1

2) Item 2

3) Item 3

ことばリスト

□製品 □機能 □特徴 □(機能が)優れる □文房具 □台所用品 □生活用品 □消す □温度
せいひん　　きのう　　とくちょう　　きのう　すぐ　　　ぶんぼうぐ　　だいどころようひん　せいかつようひん　　け　　おんど

□蛍光ペン □種類 □高温 □注意 □圧力 □(ご飯を)炊く □現在 □ふっくら □保温 □自動
けいこう　　しゅるい　こうおん　ちゅうい　あつりょく　はん　た　　げんざい　　　　　　　ほおん　　じどう

□炊き分け □調理 □(機能が)付く □温める □(ふとんを)かける □調節する □形 □気をつける
た　わ　　　ちょうり　　きのう　つ　　あたた　　　　　　　　　　　　ちょうせつ　かたち　き

2 分けてみよう Categorizing

Write the keywords in the appropriate categories.

消せるペン	圧力 IH 炊飯器	こたつ
A		

A. えんぴつと同じように消せる。
B. お米がふっくらとおいしく炊ける。
C. 何度でも書いたり消したりできる。
D. お米によって炊き方が変えられる。
こめ　　　　た　かた　か

E. 温度が調節できる。
おんど　ちょうせつ

F. 足や体を温められる。
あし　からだ　あたた

G. 保温できる。
ほおん

H. パンやケーキ、シチューやカレーなどが作れる。

Activity 4 ペアでシェアしよう Pair Share

Share your understanding from the previous activities with your partner.

例) こたつの機能は、温度が調節できることです。

Activity 5 グループでシェアしよう Group Share

Converse with your group members about the topic in Japanese.

例) こたつの機能は、温度が調節できることです。

Activity 6
質問に答えよう Respond to the Questions

Answer the following questions based on what you have read about the topic.

例）こたつには、どんな機能がありますか。

温度が調節できます。

1）消せるペンには、どんな機能がありますか。

2）圧力 IH 炊飯器には、どんな機能がありますか。

3）ペン型はさみには、どんな機能がありますか。

3 アイデアを交換しよう Communicate Ideas

Activity 7
文法パターンを見つけよう Let's Explore Language Structure!

1 聞いてみよう Let's Listen!

PPT

Listen to Sensei's presentation and jot down key ideas.

2 新しい文法パターンは？ Where is a New Language Structure?

What is the common language structure? Highlight below.

- 消せるペンは、えんぴつと同じように消せます。
- 圧力 IH 炊飯器は、お米がふっくらとおいしく炊けます。
- こたつは、温度が調節できます。

3 意味は？ What Could It Mean?

Discuss possible meanings of the language structure as a class.

4 使い方は？ How Can We Use It?

Discuss possible ways to use the language structure as a class.

5 使ってみよう Let's Use the New Language Structure!

Use the language structure in new situations.

製品	どんなことができる？
例）こたつ	足や体を温められる。
1）ペン型はさみ	
2）魚焼きグリル	
3）__________	

Activity 8 書いてみよう Write It Out

Express your ideas in writing using the new language structure.

私が使ってみたい日本の製品

製品	機能や特徴
1.	
2.	
3.	

Activity 9 ペアでシェアしよう Pair Share

Share your ideas with your partner using the writings from the previous activity.

例）A: 使ってみたい日本の製品は何ですか。その製品の機能や特徴を教えてください。

B: こたつです。こたつは、足や体を温めることができます。

______さんが使ってみたい日本の製品

製品	機能や特徴
1.	
2.	
3.	

Activity 10 まとめてみよう Organize Discussion

Organize your discussion with your partner in Japanese.

Activity 11
ディスカッションしよう Group Discussion

Discuss the topic in groups in Japanese. Use the graphic organizer to capture members' ideas, opinions, and feelings. As you listen to members' ideas, jot down key information in the graphic organizer. Finally, write down the commonalities in the middle section.

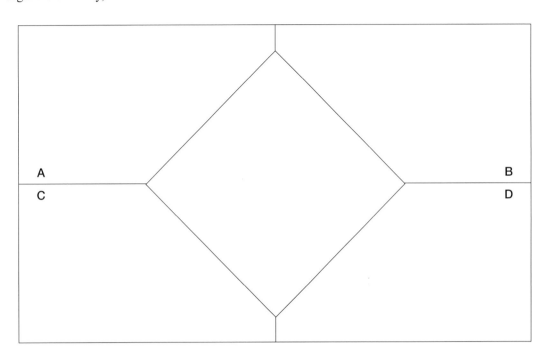

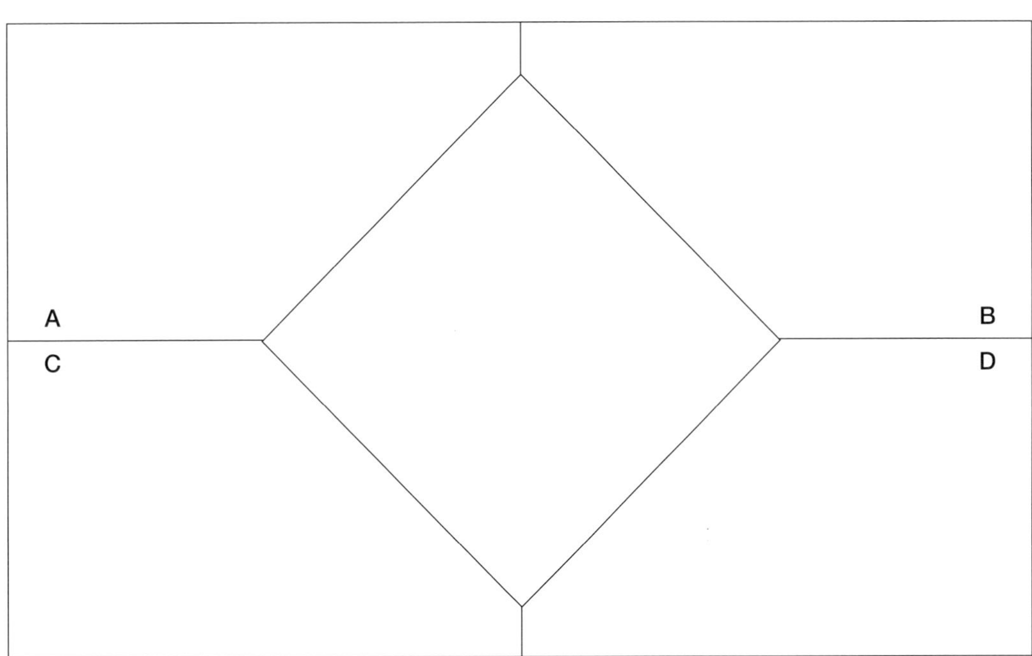

Activity 12
すらすら読もう Read Fluently

Read the article (Activity 3) to your partner. Pay attention to pronunciation, intonation, and tempo as you read aloud.

Activity 13
要約しよう Let's Summarize!

Summarize the article(s) in Japanese.

日本語でやってみよう Let's Show What We Can Do!

私が使ってみたい日本の製品

Japanese Products I Want to Use (Report)

In this cycle, you have learned about various Japanese products. You are invited to upload your blog to Japanese Costomer Report. Choose top one Japanese products that you wish to use and describe its functions and characteristics. Also, describe when you would use the product, who you would recommend it to, and any pros or cons of the product.

製品の名前と絵
機能と特徴
どんなときに使う？
どうして選んだ？

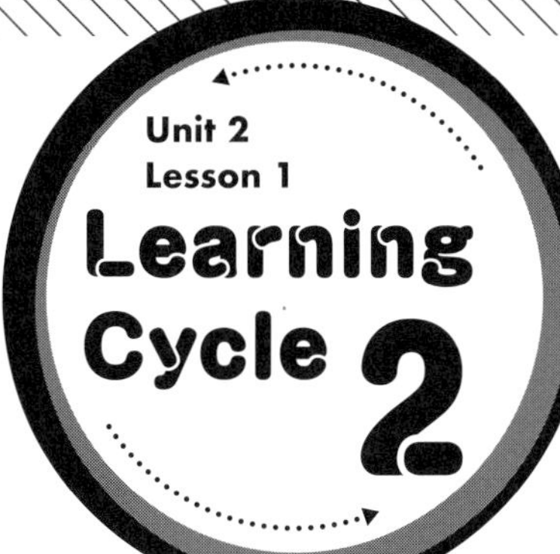

製品を選ぶ基準

せいひん　えら　きじゅん

Criteria to Choose Products

How does culture influence design? What does it take to make an attractive product? In this learning cycle, you will first examine the needs and wants of the consumer by evaluating Japanese products and products in your country. Then, you will evaluate various products using your chosen criteria. Finally, you will write a short sales pitch for your chosen item describing its characteristics and functions.

0 考えてみよう Let's Explore!

What ideas come to your mind when you think about the topic? What elements are usually mentioned for product evaluations on shopping sites?

製品を選ぶ基準

せいひん　えら　きじゅん

1 探ってみよう Investigate the World

Activity 1 文化の窓 Take a Look into Japanese Culture

Listen to Sensei's presentation twice. First, take notes on general ideas in English. When you listen a second time, jot down keywords in Japanese.

製品を選ぶ基準 Criteria to Choose Products

What is this information about?	
Keywords in Japanese	

Activity 2 まとめてみよう Graphic Organizer

Demonstrate your understanding of the previous presentation by organizing your ideas below.

2 いろいろな視点を学ぼう Recognize Diverse Perspectives

Activity 3 読んで学ぼう Read and Learn

1 読んでみよう Let's Read!

Read and annotate the article below. Then, answer the following comprehension questions.

製品を選ぶ基準 Criteria to Choose Products

みなさんは、日本の製品について、どんなイメージを持っていますか。世界中で日本の製品は、品質が高いと言われています。そして、デザインも機能も高い評価を受けているようです。

でも、製品を買うときは「値段」も気になります。みなさんは、製品を選ぶとき、どんなことを重視していますか。「値段」でしょうか。それとも「品質」でしょうか。

品質がいいかどうかは、その製品やサービスが、利用者の期待以上かどうかで決まります。値段に合う価値があるかどうかは、とても重要なことです。そのため、買う前に、その製品の評判をチェックするという人も多いでしょう。

機能的かどうか、安全かどうか、長持ちするかどうかのほかに、使いやすいかどうか、デザインがいいかどうかも、製品選びの重要なポイントです。

何を重視するかは、年齢や生活スタイルによって、違います。長く大切に使えるものを選びたいですね。

1) What kind of images do people have about Japanese products?

2) What should people do before buy products?

3) What are the other important criteria to choose products?

ことばリスト

☐基準 ☐品質 ☐評価 ☐(評価を)受ける ☐値段 ☐重視する ☐期待 ☐～以上 ☐価値(がある)
☐重要 ☐評判 ☐機能的 ☐安全 ☐長持ちする ☐年齢

2 ランキング Ranking

Write the keywords in the order of your preference or importance.

1.
2.
3.
4.
5.
6.
7.

- 品質(ひんしつ)がいい
- 値段(ねだん)に合(あ)っている
- 評判(ひょうばん)がいい
- 機能的(きのうてき)
- 安全(あんぜん)
- 長持(ながも)ちする
- 使(つか)いやすい

Activity 4 ペアでシェアしよう Pair Share

Share your understanding from the previous activities with your partner.

例(れい)) 私(わたし)にとって、デザインがいいかどうかはとても重要(じゅうよう)です。

Activity 5 グループでシェアしよう Group Share

Converse with your group members about the topic in Japanese.

例(れい)) 私(わたし)にとって、デザインがいいかどうかはとても重要(じゅうよう)です。

Activity 6
質問に答えよう Respond to the Questions

Answer the following questions based on what you have read about the topic.

例) シャープペンシルを選ぶとき、何が重要ですか。

私にとって、書きやすいかどうかはとても重要です。

1) 車を選ぶとき、何が重要ですか。

2) 洋服を選ぶとき、何が重要ですか。

3) ゲームを選ぶとき、何が重要ですか。

4) ＿＿＿＿＿＿＿＿とき、何が重要ですか。

3 アイデアを交換しよう Communicate Ideas

Activity 7
文法パターンを見つけよう Let's Explore Language Structure!

1 聞いてみよう Let's Listen!

PPT

Listen to Sensei's presentation and jot down key ideas.

2 新しい文法パターンは？ Where is a New Language Structure?

What is the common language structure? Highlight below.

- 製品を選ぶとき、値段に合う価値があるかどうかは、とても重要なことです。
- 製品を選ぶとき、機能的かどうか、安全かどうかは、重要なポイントです。
- デザインがいいかどうかも、製品選びの重要なポイントです。

3 意味は？ What Could It Mean?

Discuss possible meanings of the language structure as a class.

4 使い方は？ How Can We Use It?

Discuss possible ways to use the language structure as a class.

5 使ってみよう Let's Use the New Language Structure!

Use the language structure in new situations.

例）（大学を選ぶ）➡ 大学を選ぶとき、有名かどうかはとても重要です。

1）（仕事を選ぶ）➡ ……………………

2）（パートナーを選ぶ）➡ ……………………

3）（＿＿＿＿を選ぶ）➡ ……………………

Activity 8 書いてみよう Write It Out

Express your ideas in writing using the new language structure.

私の製品選びの重要なポイント

何が重要？	理由
1.	
2.	
3.	

Activity 9
ペアでシェアしよう Pair Share

Share your ideas with your partner using the writings from the previous activity.

例) A: 製品選びの重要なポイントは何ですか。それは、どうしてですか。

B: 私にとって、デザインがいいかどうかはとても重要です。なぜなら、ずっと使えるからです。

__________さんの製品選びの重要なポイント

何が重要？	理由
1.	
2.	
3.	

Activity 10
まとめてみよう Organize Discussion

Organize your discussion with your partner in Japanese.

Activity 11
ディスカッションしよう　Group Discussion

Discuss the topic in groups in Japanese. Use the graphic organizer to capture members' ideas, opinions, and feelings. As you listen to members' ideas, jot down key information in the graphic organizer. Finally, write down the commonalities in the middle section.

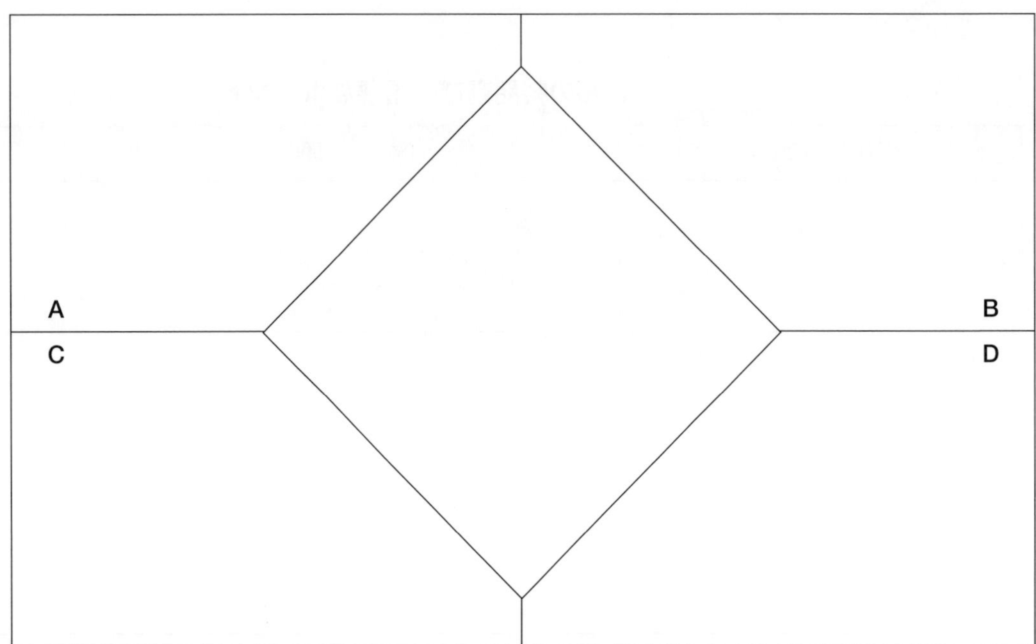

Activity 12
すらすら読もう　Read Fluently

Read the article (Activity 3) to your partner. Pay attention to pronunciation, intonation, and tempo as you read aloud.

Activity 13
要約しよう　Let's Summarize!

Summarize the article(s) in Japanese.

4 日本語でやってみよう Let's Show What We Can Do!

おすすめの製品(せいひん) Product Recommendation (Sales Pitch)

In this cycle, you have evaluated various Japanese products and products in your country using your chosen criteria. You are invited to submit your sales pitch to a Japanese radio station. Write a short sales pitch for one item of your choice by describing its characteristics and functions. Begin your pitch by appealing to consumers' emotions. Then, describe how this product can improve their life.

おすすめの製品(せいひん)：

Reference: List of Criteria

□ 品質(ひんしつ)がいい	□ 値段(ねだん)に合(あ)っている	□ 評判(ひょうばん)がいい
□ 機能的(きのうてき)	□ 安全(あんぜん)	□ 長持(ながも)ちする
□ 使(つか)いやすい	□ ________	□ ________

Unit 2 Mid Task

日本語でアクション！

Take Action in Japanese!

日本と私の国の製品

Japanese Products and My Country's Products (Comparative Report)

You are invited to be a writer for a Japanese teenager magazine. Write a report comparing and contrasting on Japanese products and your country's products. Give at least three similarities/differences, and elaborate by providing examples. Lastly, state your preference between the two, and give your reasoning. Incorporate the following structures:

Required

- ☐ ～かどうか、～
- ☐ Potential Form
- ☐ ～に比べて、～
- ☐ 私にとって、～

Optional

- ☐ 一方で、～
- ☐ ～とき、～
- ☐ ～といいです。

日本の製品と＿＿＿＿＿＿＿の製品

Unit 2 進化するデザイン Evolving Design

How does design impact our everyday lives?

Lesson 2 いいデザインの要素 Elements of Good Design

Essential Questions:

- How can good design improve our lives?
- How does design impact our everyday lives?
- How does the design reflect culture?

Can-do List:

- ☐ Define what makes "good design"
- ☐ Describe characteristics of good design
- ☐ State social and environmental contributions made by good designs
- ☐ Discuss your opinion on whether a design is good or not, and why
- ☐ Propose your own design/redesign of an existing everyday item

生活を助けるモノやサービス

Characteristics of Products and Services That Improve Our Lives

How can good design improve our lives? In this learning cycle, you will first learn various products and services that help people's lives. Then, you will discuss good design elements in small groups. Finally, you will create a collage with things and/or services that are improving the lives of your community members.

0 考えてみよう Let's Explore!

What do you notice in the title picture? (p.73) What ideas come to your mind when you think about the topic? Jot down keywords in Japanese below.

生活を助ける
モノやサービス

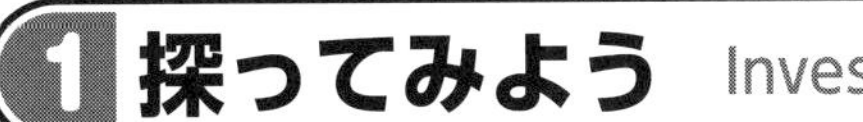

1 探ってみよう Investigate the World

Activity 1 文化の窓 Take a Look into Japanese Culture

PPT

Listen to Sensei's presentation twice. First, take notes on general ideas in English. When you listen a second time, jot down keywords in Japanese.

生活を助けるモノやサービス
Characteristics of Products and Services That Improve Our Lives

What is this information about?	
Keywords in Japanese	

Activity 2 まとめてみよう Graphic Organizer

Demonstrate your understanding of the previous presentation by organizing your ideas below.

Activity 3 読んで学ぼう Read and Learn

1 読んでみよう Let's Read!

Read and annotate the article below. Then, answer the following comprehension questions.

生活を助けるモノやサービス

Characteristics of Products and Services That Improve Our Lives

私たちの社会や生活を助けているモノやサービスには、どんなものがあるでしょうか。さまざまなモノやサービスが私たちの社会や生活を豊かにしています。

家族型ロボット

家族型ロボットは、ペットと同じように私たちに安らぎを与えてくれます。家に帰ったときに迎えてくれたり、だっこすると喜んでくれたりします。一人暮らしの高齢者が多い日本では、家族型ロボットと一緒にいるおかげで、寂しくないという人もいます。

1) Give one example of how a family companion robot helps our lives.

メガネ型スマートグラス

メガネ型スマートグラスは、今後、ビジネスや日常生活で使われるようになるでしょう。作業をするとき、リストなどがグラスに表示されます。何も持たなくても作業できるので、時間の節約になります。演劇などを見るときも、字幕がグラスに表示されるので、内容をすぐに理解することができます。これらの便利な機能のおかげで、生活がしやすくなるでしょう。

2) In what way do these glasses improve our lives?

おてらおやつクラブ

おてらおやつクラブでは、お寺にあるお菓子や果物、生活用品などのお供え物を、経済的に余裕がない家庭に分ける活動を行っています。このような活動のおかげで、多くの子どもたちが助かっています。800以上のお寺が参加していて、お寺と地域をつなぐ取り組みとして評価されています。

3) Who benefits from this service?

ことばリスト

□助ける □豊か(にする) □〜型 □安らぎ □(安らぎを)与える □迎える □だっこする □喜ぶ
□一人暮らし □高齢者 □一緒に □寂しい □今後 □日常生活 □作業(をする) □表示する
□節約(になる) □演劇 □字幕 □内容 □理解する □お供え物 □経済的 □余裕(がない)
□家庭 □活動 □助かる □地域 □つなぐ □取り組み □評価される

2 分けてみよう Categorizing

Write the keywords in the appropriate categories.

家族型ロボットのおかげで	メガネ型スマートグラスのおかげで	おてらおやつクラブのおかげで
B		

A. 字幕を見ることができます。
B. 一人暮らしの高齢者は寂しくないです。
C. 経済的に余裕がない家庭の子どもたちが助かっています。
D. 時間の節約になります。
E. 内容をすぐに理解することができます。

Activity 4 ペアでシェアしよう Pair Share

Share your understanding from the previous activities with your partner.

例) 家族型ロボットのおかげで、一人暮らしの高齢者は寂しくないです。

Activity 5 グループでシェアしよう Group Share

Converse with your group members about the topic in Japanese.

例) 家族型ロボットのおかげで、一人暮らしの高齢者は寂しくないです。

Activity 6 質問に答えよう Respond to the Questions

Answer the following questions based on what you have read about the topic.

例）家族型ロボットあると、いいことを教えてください。

家族型ロボットのおかげで、一人暮らしの高齢者は寂しくないです。

1）家族型ロボットあると、いいことを教えてください。

2）メガネ型スマートグラスがあると、いいことを教えてください。

3）おてらおやつクラブがあると、いいことを教えてください。

3 アイデアを交換しよう Communicate Ideas

Activity 7 文法パターンを見つけよう Let's Explore Language Structure!

1 聞いてみよう Let's Listen!

PPT

Listen to Sensei's presentation and jot down key ideas.

2 新しい文法パターンは？ Where is a New Language Structure?

What is the common language structure? Highlight below.

- 家族型ロボットと一緒にいるおかげで、寂しくないという人もいます。
- これらの便利な機能のおかげで、生活がしやすくなるでしょう。
- このような活動のおかげで、多くの子どもたちが助かっています。

3 意味は？ What Could It Mean?

Discuss possible meanings of the language structure as a class.

4 使い方は？ How Can We Use It?

Discuss possible ways to use the language structure as a class.

5 使ってみよう Let's Use the New Language Structure!

Use the language structure in new situations.

何のおかげで？	結果
例）パソコンのおかげで	生活が便利になりました。
1) ____________	私たちの生活はよくなりました。
2) ____________	日本語が話せるようになりました。
3) ____________	人々は助かっています。
4) ____________	社会が豊かになりました。

Activity 8 書いてみよう Write It Out

Express your ideas in writing using the new language structure.

私の意見：生活をよくしたモノやサービス

モノ・サービス	理由

Activity 9 ペアでシェアしよう Pair Share

Share your ideas with your partner using the writings from the previous activity.

例) A: 生活をよくしたモノやサービスは何ですか。それはどうしてですか。

B: 家族型ロボットです。家族型ロボットのおかげで、一人暮らしの高齢者が寂しくないからです。

＿＿＿＿＿＿さんの意見：生活をよくしたモノやサービス

モノ・サービス	理由

Activity 10 まとめてみよう Organize Discussion

Organize your discussion with your partner in Japanese.

Activity 11
ディスカッションしよう Group Discussion

Discuss the topic in groups in Japanese. Use the graphic organizer to capture members' ideas, opinions, and feelings. As you listen to members' ideas, jot down key information in the graphic organizer. Finally, write down the commonalities in the middle section.

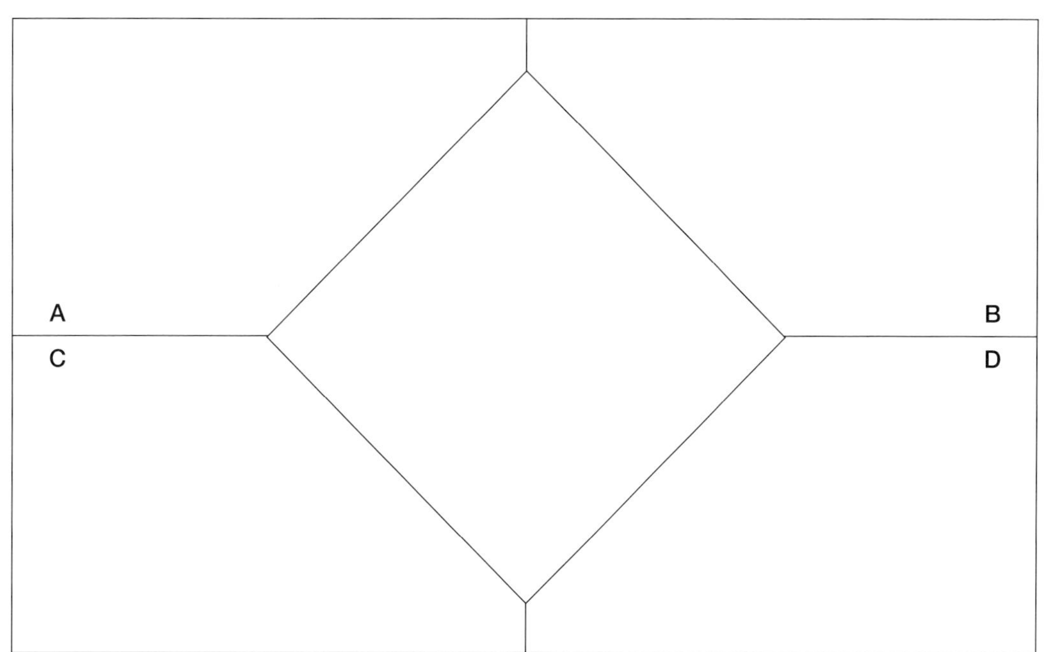

Activity 12
すらすら読もう Read Fluently

Read the article (Activity 3) to your partner. Pay attention to pronunciation, intonation, and tempo as you read aloud.

Activity 13
要約しよう Let's Summarize!

Summarize the article(s) in Japanese.

日本語でやってみよう Let's Show What We Can Do!

町で見つけたいいデザイン

まち　み

Good Design in My Community (Poster Presentation)

In this cycle, you learned about various products and services that help people's lives. Create a collage with things and/or services that are improving the lives of your community members. Present your collage to your Japanese friends by informing them about the good designs you found in your community.

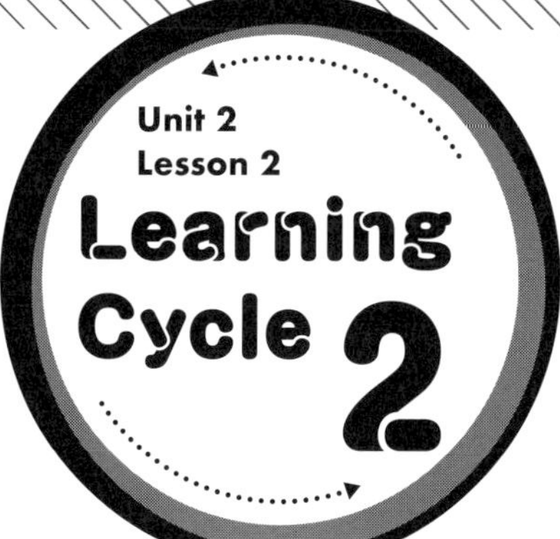

グッドデザイン賞(しょう)とは？

What is the "Good Design Award" ?

How does design impact everyday life? How does design reflect our culture? In this learning cycle, you will first learn about the requirements for the Good Design Award. Then, you will evaluate various products using those requirements. Finally, you will describe the product and reasons why the product was chosen as "Good Design Award."

0 考えてみよう Let's Explore!

What ideas come to your mind when you think about the topic? Jot down keywords in Japanese below.

いいデザイン

1 探ってみよう Investigate the World

Activity 1 文化の窓 Take a Look into Japanese Culture

Listen to Sensei's presentation twice. First, take notes on general ideas in English. When you listen a second time, jot down keywords in Japanese.

グッドデザイン賞とは？ What is the "Good Design Award"？

What is this information about?	
Keywords in Japanese	

Activity 2 まとめてみよう Graphic Organizer

Demonstrate your understanding of the previous presentation by organizing your ideas below.

2 いろいろな視点を学ぼう Recognize Diverse Perspectives

Activity 3 読んで学ぼう Read and Learn

1 読んでみよう Let's Read!

Read and annotate the article below. Then, answer the following comprehension questions.

グッドデザイン賞とは？ What is the "Good Design Award"？

日本では、１年に１回、いいデザインに「グッドデザイン賞」が贈られます。審査の対象は、生活用品や家具などの製品だけでなく、建物や都市開発、サービス、エンターテイメント、ボランティア活動など、さまざまです。

では、どんなデザインがグッドデザイン賞に選ばれるのでしょうか。いいデザインは、見た目の美しさだけでなく、社会や生活も豊かにします。グッドデザイン賞では、次のようなことも審査されます。

- デザインに最先端のテクノロジーが使われているかどうか
- デザインによって新しい価値が創造されたかどうか
- 社会的に必要かどうか
- 環境に優しいかどうか

創造されたモノやサービスによって、今まで不便だったことが便利になるだけでなく、価値観まで変わるということがあります。グッドデザイン賞は、そういうモノやサービスに贈られます。

1) What kind of products wouid receive this Award?

2) What are the criteria of the Good Design Award?

3) What does the Good Design Award contribute to our society?

□賞　□(賞を)贈る　□審査(する)　□対象　□家具　□建物　□都市開発　□さまざま　□見た目

□最先端　□創造する　□環境　□(環境に)優しい　□不便　□価値観(が変わる)

2 チェックリスト Checklist

Check off the keywords that apply to the information presented above.

家族型ロボット
（かぞくがた）

□ 見た目がいい　　□ 生活を豊かにする　　□ 生活が便利になる
（み め）　　　　（せいかつ ゆた）　　　　（せいかつ べんり）
□ 社会的に必要　　□ 最先端のテクノロジーが使われている
（しゃかいてき ひつよう）　（さいせんたん）　　　　（つか）
□ 環境に優しい　　□ 価値観が変わる
（かんきょう やさ）　（か ちかん か）

メガネ型
（がた）
スマートグラス

□ 見た目がいい　　□ 生活を豊かにする　　□ 生活が便利になる
（み め）　　　　（せいかつ ゆた）　　　　（せいかつ べんり）
□ 社会的に必要　　□ 最先端のテクノロジーが使われている
（しゃかいてき ひつよう）　（さいせんたん）　　　　（つか）
□ 環境に優しい　　□ 価値観が変わる
（かんきょう やさ）　（か ちかん か）

おてらおやつ
クラブ

□ 見た目がいい　　□ 生活を豊かにする　　□ 生活が便利になる
（み め）　　　　（せいかつ ゆた）　　　　（せいかつ べんり）
□ 社会的に必要　　□ 最先端のテクノロジーが使われている
（しゃかいてき ひつよう）　（さいせんたん）　　　　（つか）
□ 環境に優しい　　□ 価値観が変わる
（かんきょう やさ）　（か ちかん か）

Activity 4
ペアでシェアしよう Pair Share

Share your understanding from the previous activities with your partner.

例）家族型ロボットは、最先端のテクノロジーが使われているだけでなく、社会的に必
（れい）（かぞくがた）　　（さいせんたん）　　　　　　（つか）　　　　　　　　　（しゃかいてき ひつ
要です。
（よう）

Activity 5
グループでシェアしよう Group Share

Converse with your group members about the topic in Japanese.

例）家族型ロボットは、最先端のテクノロジーが使われているだけでなく、社会的に必
（れい）（かぞくがた）　　（さいせんたん）　　　　　　（つか）　　　　　　　　　（しゃかいてき ひつ
要です。
（よう）

Activity 6

質問に答えよう Respond to the Questions

Answer the following questions based on what you have read about the topic.

例）家族型ロボットは、どうして「グッドデザイン賞」に選ばれましたか。

最先端のテクノロジーが使われているだけでなく、社会的に必要だからです。

1）メガネ型スマートグラスは、どうして「グッドデザイン賞」に選ばれましたか。

2）おてらおやつクラブは、どうして「グッドデザイン賞」に選ばれましたか。

3）＿＿＿＿＿＿＿は、どうして「グッドデザイン賞」に選ばれましたか。

3 アイデアを交換しよう Communicate Ideas

Activity 7

文法パターンを見つけよう Let's Explore Language Structure!

1 聞いてみよう Let's Listen!

PPT

Listen to Sensei's presentation and jot down key ideas.

2 新しい文法パターンは？ Where is a New Language Structure?

What is the common language structure? Highlight below.

- 審査の対象は、生活用品や家具などの製品だけでなく、都市開発やボランティア活動など、さまざまです。
- いいデザインは、見た目の美しさだけでなく、社会や生活も豊かにします。
- 今まで不便だったことが便利になるだけでなく、価値観まで変わるということがあります。

3 意味は？ What Could It Mean?

Discuss possible meanings of the language structure as a class.

4 使い方は？ How Can We Use It?

Discuss possible ways to use the language structure as a class.

5 使ってみよう Let's Use the New Language Structure!

Use the language structure in new situations.

例）（スマホ）

➡ スマホはどこででも話せるだけでなく、いろいろな情報にもアクセスできます。

1)（パソコン）

➡

2)（電気自動車）

➡

3)（ロボット）

➡

4)（＿＿＿＿＿＿）

➡

Activity 8 書いてみよう Write It Out

Express your ideas in writing using the new language structure.

私の意見：「グッドデザイン賞」にしたいモノやサービス

モノやサービス	理由

Activity 9 ペアでシェアしよう Pair Share

Share your ideas with your partner using the writings from the previous activity.

例(れい)) A: どんなモノやサービスに「グッドデザイン賞(しょう)」をあげたいですか。それはどうしてですか。

B: 私(わたし)は、家族型(かぞくがた)ロボットにあげたいです。家族型(かぞくがた)ロボットは、最先端(さいせんたん)のテクノロジーが使(つか)われているだけでなく、社会的(しゃかいてき)に必要(ひつよう)だからです。

__________さんの意見(いけん)：「グッドデザイン賞(しょう)」にしたいモノやサービス

モノやサービス	理由(りゆう)

Activity 10 まとめてみよう Organize Discussion

Organize your discussion with your partner in Japanese.

Activity 11 ディスカッションしよう Group Discussion

Discuss the topic in groups in Japanese. Use the graphic organizer to capture members' ideas, opinions, and feelings. As you listen to members' ideas, jot down key information in the graphic organizer. Finally, write down the commonalities in the middle section.

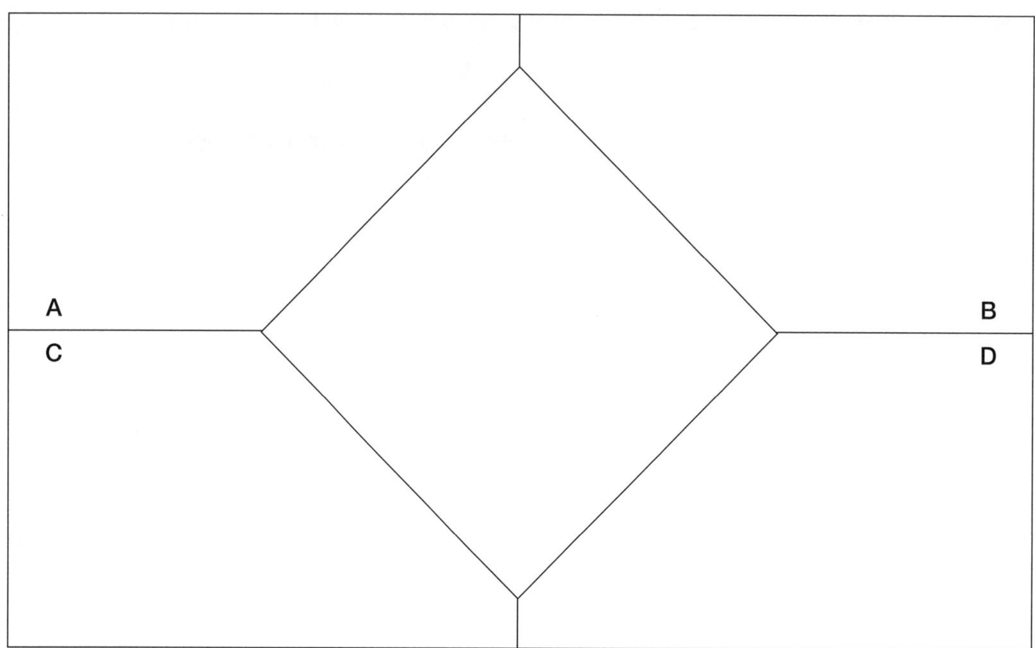

Activity 12 すらすら読(よ)もう Read Fluently

Read the article (Activity 3) to your partner. Pay attention to pronunciation, intonation, and tempo as you read aloud.

Activity 13 要約(ようやく)しよう Let's Summarize!

Summarize the article(s) in Japanese.

4 日本語でやってみよう Let's Show What We Can Do!

グッドデザイン賞に選ばれた理由

Reasons for Good Design Award (Report)

In this cycle, you learned about the requirements for the Good Design Award and evaluated various products using those requirements. You are invited to write a report to review as a guest user of a prodcut. Describe the product and reasons why the product was chosen as "Good Design Award."

Required

- ☐ ～だけでなく、～
- ☐ ～おかげで、～
- ☐ 私にとって、～

Optional

- ☐ ～かどうか、～
- ☐ Potential Form
- ☐ ～とき、～

Unit 2 Final Task

日本語でアクション！

Take Action in Japanese!

グッドデザイン賞をめざそう！

Task Sheet & Rubrics 

Aim for the Good Design Award!

How does design impact our daily lives? Your task is to design or redesign existing everyday items to improve our lives as well as Japanese people's lives. Introduce your design by creating a poster or pamphlet and submit to the team at the Good Design Award.

Your Role & Purpose	Designer to improve everyday items
Your Audience	Good Design Award Selection Committee
Language	☐ Describe characteristics and functions of the product ☐ Address improvements by comparing to the previous design ☐ Explain why the design appeals to Japanese sense of aesthetics ☐ Describe contributions to everyday lives of Japanese people ☐ Give multiple reasons why the product deserves the award
Product	**Product Type:** Poster/pamphlet/slideshow ☐ Hand-drawn or digital ☐ Presentation (e.g., gallery walk)

Unit 3 日本芸術(にほんげいじゅつ)への響(ひび)き Be Inspired by Japanese Art

How does art in Japan reflect its culture?

Lesson 1 美術(びじゅつ)の楽(たの)しみ方(かた) How to Enjoy Art

Essential Questions:

- What are the characteristics of traditional Japanese art?
- How does art reflect our society?
- How does art enrich our lives?
- How do art forms differ depending on the country?
- How do people interpret and appreciate art?

Can-do List:

Check!

- ☐ Identify characteristics of Japanese woodblock prints and visual arts
- ☐ Share interpretations of various artworks in groups
- ☐ Give a short cultural perspective presentation about a Japanese art form of my choice

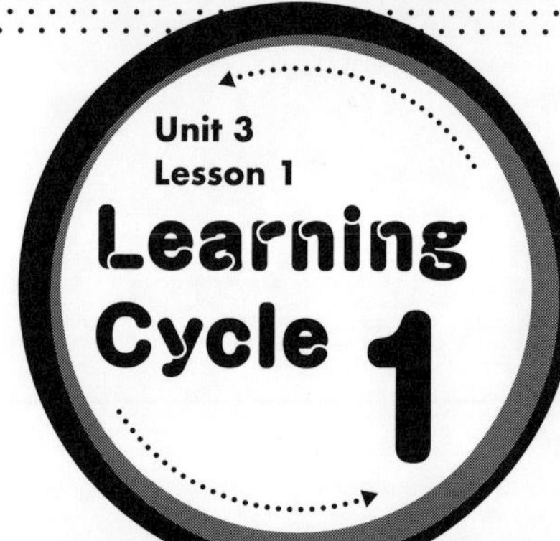

浮世絵とは？

What is *Ukiyo-e*?

What are the characteristics of traditional Japanese art? How does art reflect our society? In this learning cycle, first you will learn about a traditional Japanese art, *Ukiyo-e*, and famous *Ukiyo-e* artists highlighting their unique artistic expressions. Then, you will discuss your thoughts and feelings about their art in small groups. Finally, you will write an article about aspects of Japanese art in order to introduce the piece to Japanese friends.

0 考えてみよう Let's Explore!

What do you notice in the title picture? (p.93) What ideas come to your mind when you think about the topic? Jot down keywords in Japanese below.

日本のアート

1 探ってみよう Investigate the World

Activity 1 文化の窓（ぶんかのまど） Take a Look into Japanese Culture

Listen to Sensei's presentation twice. First, take notes on general ideas in English. When you listen a second time, jot down keywords in Japanese.

浮世絵（うきよえ）とは？ What is *Ukiyo-e*?

What is this information about?	
Keywords in Japanese	

Activity 2 まとめてみよう Graphic Organizer

Demonstrate your understanding of the previous presentation by organizing your ideas below.

2 いろいろな視点を学ぼう Recognize Diverse Perspectives

Activity 3 読んで学ぼう（よんでまなぼう） Read and Learn

1 読んでみよう（よんでみよう） Let's Read!

Read and annotate the article below. Then, answer the following comprehension questions.

浮世絵とは？ What is *Ukiyo-e*?

浮世絵とは、江戸時代（1603年-1868年）に流行した版画絵のことです。版画絵は、まず紙に絵を描きます。次に、その絵を木に彫って、最後に色を付けて刷ります。簡単に同じ絵がたくさん作れるので、人気が出ました。

浮世絵には、人物だけでなく、風景や動物なども描かれています。浮世絵は、今でいうと、スポーツ選手のカードやポストカードと同じです。有名な画家には、葛飾北斎や歌川広重などがいます。

葛飾北斎の有名な作品に「冨嶽三十六景」があります。その中でも、「神奈川沖浪裏」は有名で、今でもとても人気があります。巨大な波は生き物のようで、今にも船を飲み込みそうです。

歌川広重は、雨や雪が本当に降っているように、自然をリアルに描いた画家です。絵を見ていると、雨の音や雪を踏む音だけが聞こえてくるような静けさを感じます。

浮世絵は、ゴッホやセザンヌなど、ヨーロッパで活躍した画家たちにも大きな影響を与えました。

❶ 葛飾北斎
「冨嶽三十六景 神奈川沖浪裏」

❷ 歌川広重
「名所江戸百景 大はしあたけの夕立」

1) What is *Ukiyo-e*?

2) What were the subjects of *Ukiyo-e*?

3) What are the names of some famous *Ukiyo-e* artists and the characteristics of their work?

4) List names of worldly known artists who were influenced by *Ukiyo-e*.

ことばリスト 

□流行する □版画絵 □紙 □(絵を)描く □彫る □(色を)付ける □(版画絵を)刷る □人物
□風景 □画家 □巨大 □波 □生き物 □今にも □飲み込む □自然 □音 □踏む □静けさ
□活躍する

2 マッチング Matching

Match the keywords and pictures or descriptions below.

❸ 葛飾北斎
かつしかほくさい
「冨嶽三十六景 凱風快晴」
ふ がくさんじゅうろっけい がいふうかいせい
例） F
れい

❹ 歌川広重
うたがわひろしげ
「東海道五十三次 蒲原夜之雪」
とうかいどう ご じゅうさんつぎ かんばらよる の ゆき
1）

❺ 歌川広重
うたがわひろしげ
「名所江戸百景
めいしょ え ど ひゃっけい
逆井のわたし」
さかさ い
2）

❻ 歌川広重
うたがわひろしげ
「東海道五十三次 日本橋朝之景」
とうかいどう ご じゅうさんつぎ にほんばしあさ の けい
3）

❼ 歌川広重
うたがわひろしげ
「東海道五十三次 庄野白雨」
とうかいどう ご じゅうさんつぎ しょう の はくう
4）

❽ 葛飾北斎
かつしかほくさい
「諸国滝廻り
しょこくたきめぐ
下野黒髪山
しもつけくろかみやま
きりふりの滝」
たき
5）

A. 雨の音が聞こえてくるようだ。
B. 雪を踏む音が聞こえてくるようだ。
C. 水の音が聞こえてくるようだ。
D. 鳥の声が聞こえてくるようだ。
E. 人々の声が聞こえてくるようだ。
ひとびと こえ き

F. 山が燃えているようだ。
やま も

Activity 4

ペアでシェアしよう Pair Share

Share your understanding from the previous activities with your partner.

例） ❶の絵は、巨大な波が生き物のようです。

Activity 5

グループでシェアしよう Group Share

Converse with your group members about the topic in Japanese.

例） ❶の絵は、巨大な波が生き物のようです。

Activity 6
質問に答えよう Respond to the Questions

Answer the following questions based on what you have read about the topic.

例）❶の絵について、感想を教えてください。
巨大な波は、まるで生き物のようです。

1）❷の絵について、感想を教えてください。

2）❸の絵について、感想を教えてください。

3）＿＿＿の絵について、感想を教えてください。

3 アイデアを交換しよう Communicate Ideas

Activity 7
文法パターンを見つけよう Let's Explore Language Structure!

1 聞いてみよう Let's Listen!

PPT

Listen to Sensei's presentation and jot down key ideas.

2 新しい文法パターンは？ Where is a New Language Structure?

What is the common language structure? Highlight below.

- 巨大な波は生き物のようで、今にも船を飲み込みそうです。
- 歌川広重は、雨や雪が本当に降っているように、自然をリアルに描いた画家です。
- 雨の音や雪を踏む音だけが聞こえてくるような静けさを感じます。

3 意味は？ What Could It Mean?

Discuss possible meanings of the language structure as a class.

4 使い方は？ How Can We Use It?

Discuss possible ways to use the language structure as a class.

5 使ってみよう Let's Use the New Language Structure!

Use the language structure in new situations.

例）子どもがさるのように木に登っています。

1) 本が机の上に＿＿＿＿＿＿＿＿ありります。

2) お母さんが＿＿＿＿＿＿＿＿怒っています。

3) お父さんが＿＿＿＿＿＿＿＿寝ています。

Activity 8 書いてみよう Write It Out

Express your ideas in writing using the new language structure.

私が選んだ絵

タイトル

＿＿＿＿＿＿＿＿＿＿＿＿

画家
説明・感想

Activity 9 ペアでシェアしよう Pair Share

Share your ideas with your partner using the writings from the previous activity.

例) A: だれの絵を選びましたか。その絵のタイトルは何ですか。感想を教えてください。
B: 葛飾北斎の「神奈川沖浪裏」を選びました。巨大な波は、まるで生き物のようです。

＿＿＿＿＿さんが選んだ絵

タイトル

＿＿＿＿＿＿＿＿＿＿＿＿＿＿

画家
説明・感想

Activity 10 まとめてみよう Organize Discussion

Organize your discussion with your partner in Japanese.

Activity 11
ディスカッションしよう　Group Discussion

Discuss the topic in groups in Japanese. Use the graphic organizer to capture members' ideas, opinions, and feelings. As you listen to members' ideas, jot down key information in the graphic organizer. Finally, write down the commonalities in the middle section.

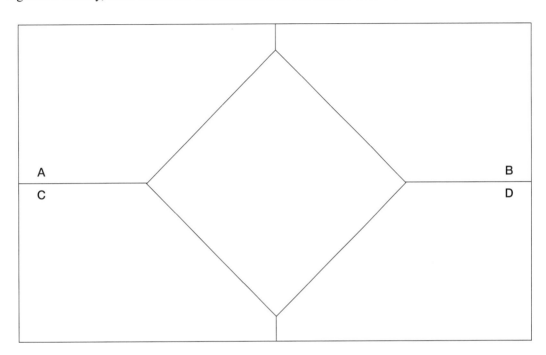

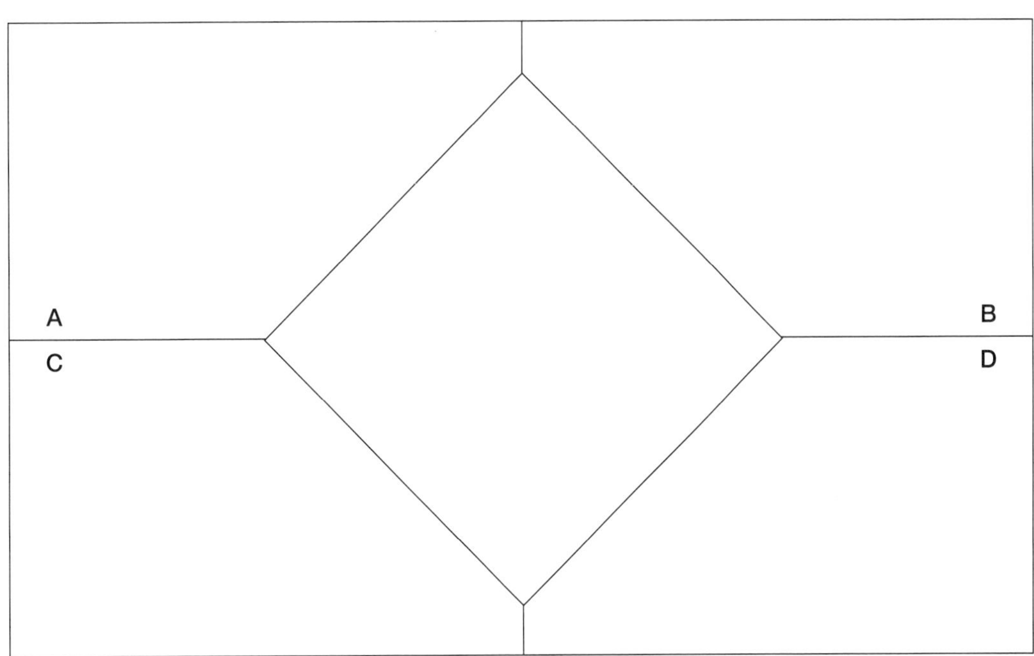

Activity 12
すらすら読もう　Read Fluently

Read the article (Activity 3) to your partner. Pay attention to pronunciation, intonation, and tempo as you read aloud.

Activity 13
要約しよう　Let's Summarize!

Summarize the article(s) in Japanese.

4 日本語でやってみよう Let's Show What We Can Do!

お気に入りの日本の美術品 My Favorite Japanese Art (Opinion)

In this learning cycle, you learned about *Ukiyo-e* and famous *Ukiyo-e* artists. Choose one Japanese art piece and write about 5 aspects about this piece. Then, introduce it to Japanese friends. You must explain your interpretation of the piece, as well as your impression of it. Upload your final writing with the picture of your art piece on an online post.

Required

- □ ～よう
- □ 私の感想としては、～
- □ ～と思います。

Optional

- □ しかし、～
- □ 一方で、～
- □ ～に比べて、～
- □ なぜなら／その理由は、～からです。

美術品 ______________________

美術家 ______________________

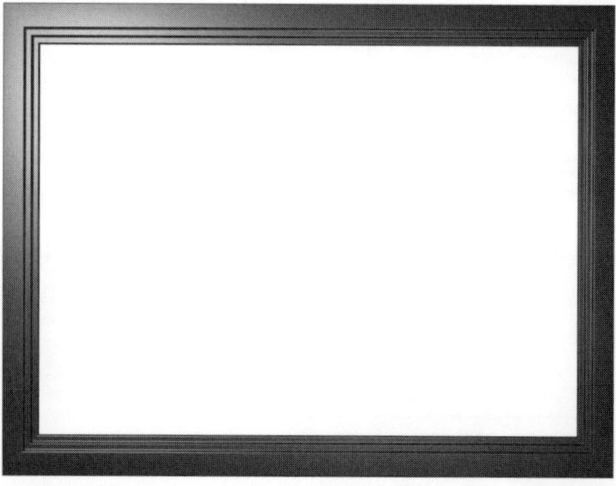

説明・感想

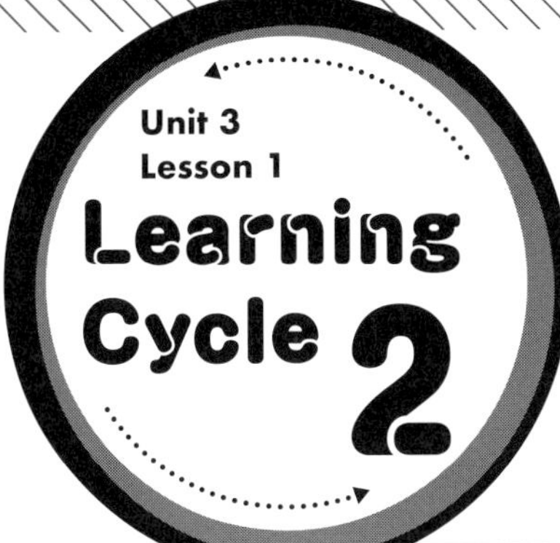

美術鑑賞（びじゅつかんしょう）

Art Appreciation

How does art enrich our lives? How do people interpret and appreciate art? In this learning cycle, you will first read a sample art appreciation conversation between a director of a museum and high school students. Then, you will engage in art appreciation with your classmates by giving your interpretation and impression of various art pieces. Lastly, you will choose one piece and create your own art appreciation in writing.

0 考えてみよう Let's Explore!

What ideas come to your mind when you think about the topic? Jot down keywords in Japanese below.

美術鑑賞（びじゅつかんしょう）

1 探ってみよう Investigate the World

Activity 1 文化の窓 Take a Look into Japanese Culture

Listen to Sensei's presentation twice. First, take notes on general ideas in English. When you listen a second time, jot down keywords in Japanese.

美術鑑賞 Art Appriciation

What is this information about?	
Keywords in Japanese	

Activity 2 まとめてみよう Graphic Organizer

Demonstrate your understanding of the previous presentation by organizing your ideas below.

2 いろいろな視点を学ぼう Recognize Diverse Perspectives

Activity 3 読んで学ぼう Read and Learn

1 読んでみよう Let's Read!

Read and annotate the article below. Then, answer the following comprehension questions.

美術鑑賞 Art appreciation

10

❶ ゴッホ「夜のカフェテラス」

館長：これは、オランダの有名な画家ゴッホが1888年に描いた「夜のカフェテラス」という絵です。ゴッホが南フランスのアルルという町に住んでいたときに描いたそうです。みなさん、この絵を見た感想を聞かせてください。

学生A：夜なのにカフェテラスがとても明るくて、楽しくおしゃべりする人の声や食器の音が聞こえてくるような気がします。

館長：そうですね。夜空の濃い青と星やカフェの黄色い明かりのコントラストがとても美しく、強く印象に残る作品ですね。ほかにはどうですか。

学生B：町の中心にあって、たくさんの人が集まる居心地のいいカフェを表現しているような気がします。

館長：そうですね。今でも同じようなカフェがあって、多くの観光客が訪れているそうです。あなたはどうですか。

学生C：じっと見ていると、19世紀のこの時代にタイムスリップしたような気がします。このカフェに行きたくなります。

館長：いろいろな感想があって、おもしろいですね。一枚の絵から、いろいろなことが想像できるので、今後も美術鑑賞をぜひ続けてください。

1) What were the students' impressions of this Gogh's artwork?

A :

B :

C :

2) Summarize Gogh's artwork information here.

3) What is the director of the museum's hope?

ことばリスト 

☐美術鑑賞 ☐館長 ☐感想 ☐おしゃべりする ☐食器 ☐夜空 ☐濃い ☐星 ☐明かり

☐印象（に残る） ☐作品 ☐中心 ☐居心地（のいい） ☐表現する ☐観光客 ☐訪れる ☐じっと見る

☐～世紀

2 マッチング Matching

Match the keywords and pictures or descriptions below.

*Refer to the colored pictures on page 112.

❷ ゴッホ
「ひまわり」
例) D

❸ ルノワール
「ピアノに寄る少女たち」
1) ________

❹ ムンク
「叫び」
2) ________

❺ モネ
「ラ・ジャポネーズ」
3) ________

A. 悲しみや苦しみが伝わってくるような気がする。
B. 浮世絵の影響を受けているような気がする。
C. 話し声やピアノの音が聞こえてくるような気がする。
D. 黄色が太陽の光や希望を表しているような気がする。

Activity 4 ペアでシェアしよう Pair Share

Share your understanding from the previous activities with your partner.

例) ❶の絵は、夜なのにカフェテラスがとても明るくて、楽しくおしゃべりする人の声や食器の音が聞こえてくるような気がします。

Activity 5 グループでシェアしよう Group Share

Converse with your group members about the topic in Japanese.

例) ❶の絵は、夜なのにカフェテラスがとても明るくて、楽しくおしゃべりする人の声や食器の音が聞こえてくるような気がします。

Activity 6 質問に答えよう Respond to the Questions

Answer the following questions based on what you have read about the topic.

例) ❶の絵について、感想を教えてください。
楽しくおしゃべりする人の声や食器の音が聞こえてくるような気がします。

1) ❷の絵について、感想を教えてください。

2) ❸の絵について、感想を教えてください。

3) ＿＿＿の絵について、感想を教えてください。

3 アイデアを交換しよう Communicate Ideas

Activity 7 文法パターンを見つけよう Let's Explore Language Structure!

1 聞いてみよう Let's Listen!

PPT

Listen to Sensei's presentation and jot down key ideas.

2 新しい文法パターンは？ Where is a New Language Structure?

What is the common language structure? Highlight below.

- 楽しくおしゃべりする人の声や食器の音が聞こえてくるような気がします。
- たくさんの人が集まる居心地のいいカフェを表現しているような気がします。
- 19 世紀のこの時代にタイムスリップしたような気がします。

3 意味は？ What Could It Mean?

Discuss possible meanings of the language structure as a class.

4 使い方は？ How Can We Use It?

Discuss possible ways to use the language structure as a class.

5 使ってみよう Let's Use the New Language Structure!

Use the language structure in new situations.

例）ネコの鳴き声が聞こえるような気がします。

1) ....

2) ....

3) ....

Activity 8

書いてみよう Write It Out

Express your ideas in writing using the new language structure.

私が選んだ絵

タイトル

____

画家
説明・感想

Activity 9

ペアでシェアしよう Pair Share

Share your ideas with your partner using the writings from the previous activity.

例) A: だれの絵を選びましたか。その絵のタイトルは何ですか。感想を教えてください。
B: ゴッホの「夜のカフェテラス」を選びました。夜なのにカフェテラスがとても明るくて、楽しくおしゃべりする人の声や食器の音が聞こえてくるような気がします。

__________さんが選んだ絵

タイトル

____

画家

説明・感想

Activity 10

まとめてみよう Organize Discussion

Organize your discussion with your partner in Japanese.

Activity 11
ディスカッションしよう Group Discussion

Discuss the topic in groups in Japanese. Use the graphic organizer to capture members' ideas, opinions, and feelings. As you listen to members' ideas, jot down key information in the graphic organizer. Finally, write down the commonalities in the middle section.

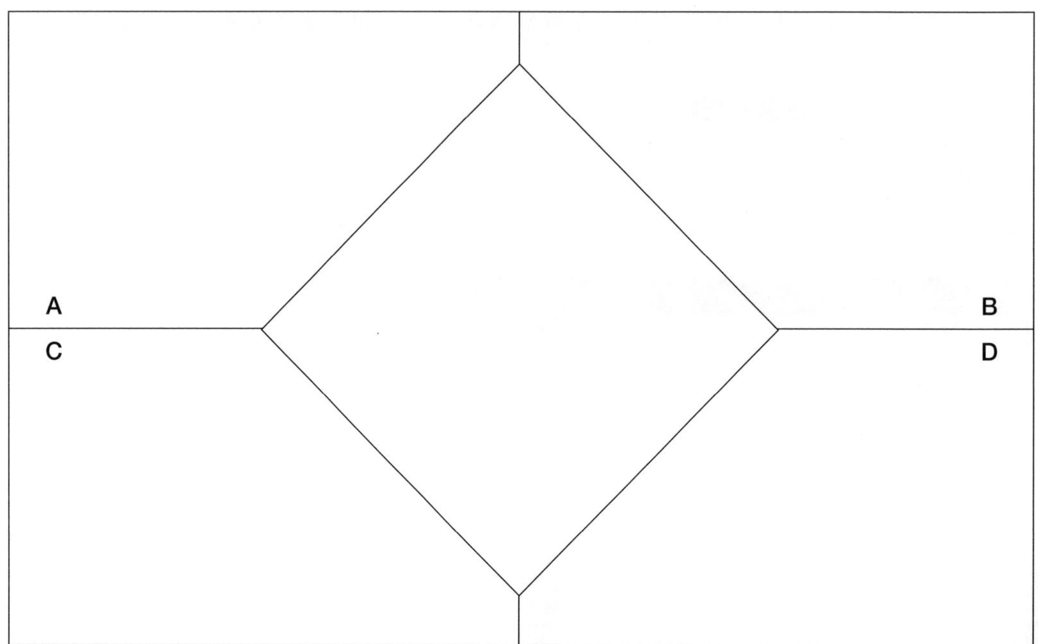

Activity 12
すらすら読もう Read Fluently

Read the article (Activity 3) to your partner. Pay attention to pronunciation, intonation, and tempo as you read aloud.

Activity 13
要約しよう Let's Summarize!

Summarize the article(s) in Japanese.

4 日本語でやってみよう Let's Show What We Can Do!

お気に入りの世界の美術品

Art Around the World (Commentary)

In this learning cycle, you learned about and engaged in art appreciation with your classmates by giving your interpretation and impression of various art pieces. Choose one of the art pieces introduced in this unit and write an art appreciation post to an art museum website about it. You must explain your interpretation of the piece, as well as your impression of it.

Required

- ☐ ～ような気がします。
- ☐ ～よう

Optional

- ☐ まず／最初に、～
- ☐ 次に、～
- ☐ 私の感想としては、～
- ☐ ～と思います。

美術品 ______________________

美術家 ______________________

説明・感想

Unit 3 Mid Task

日本語でアクション！

Take Action in Japanese!

日本の美術について

Japanese Art (Cultural Perspective Presentation)

You are entering an online speech contest in Japan. Research a Japanese visual art form of your choice. It may be contemporary or traditional. Talk about 3-5 aspects regarding the form of Japanese art you chosen. You have 4 minutes to prepare and 2 minutes for your presentation. Use the space below to make notes (it should not be a script of your presentation!).

*These pictures are also used in Activity 3-2.

❷ ゴッホ
「ひまわり」

❸ ルノワール
「ピアノに寄る少女たち」

❹ ムンク
「叫び」

❺ モネ
「ラ・ジャポネーズ」

Unit 3 日本芸術への響き Be Inspired by Japanese Art

How does art in Japan reflect its culture?

Lesson 2 文化体験 Cultural Experience

Essential Questions:

- What does *Sumie* convey?
- How is it relevant in our modern life?
- What is the philosophy of *Sado*, the Japanese tea ceremony?

Can-do List:

Check!

- ☐ Identify and describe the process of Japanese ink wash paintings, and experience creating one firsthand
- ☐ Identify characteristics of *Sado*
- ☐ Create an original piece of art to express your relationship with Japan

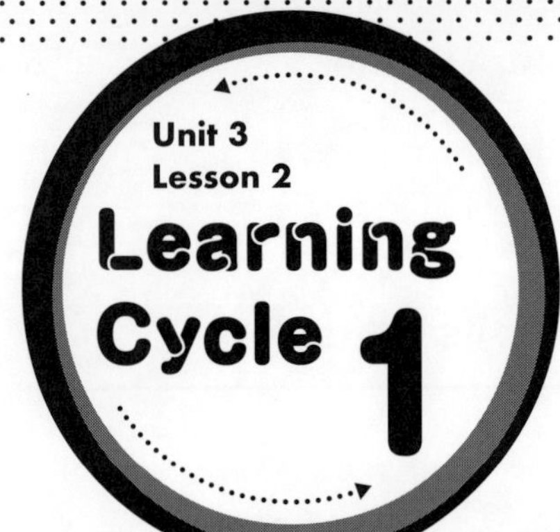

墨絵の描き方

How to Draw *Sumie*

What does Sumie convey? How is this relevant to our modern life? In this learning cycle, you will first learn about the beauty and process of creating *Sumie*. Then, you will discuss in groups the steps to skillfully draw *Sumie*. Lastly, you will have firsthand experience creating your own piece! Then, you will write a report about your experience.

0 考えてみよう Let's Explore!

1 What do you notice in the title picture? (p.113) What ideas come to your mind when you think about the topic? Jot down keywords in Japanese below.

日本文化体験

2 What forms of Japanese art do you know and are you interested in trying?

1 探ってみよう Investigate the World

Activity 1 文化の窓 Take a Look into Japanese Culture

PPT

Listen to Sensei's presentation twice. First, take notes on general ideas in English. When you listen a second time, jot down keywords in Japanese.

墨絵の描き方 How to Draw *Sumie*

What is this information about?	
Keywords in Japanese	

Activity 2 まとめてみよう Graphic Organizer

Demonstrate your understanding of the previous presentation by organizing your ideas below.

2 いろいろな視点を学ぼう Recognize Diverse Perspectives

Activity 3 読んで学ぼう Read and Learn

1 読んでみよう Let's Read!

Read and annotate the article below. Then, answer the following comprehension questions.

墨絵の描き方 How to Draw *Sumie*

墨絵とは、墨の濃淡だけで描く絵です。墨で描かれた部分と同じくらい、何も描かれてない「余白」の部分も大切です。日本人は昔から「絵が描かれた」部分を楽しみながら、余白や空間にも「美」を見つけてきました。それでは、一緒に墨絵を描いてみましょう！

＜必要な道具＞ 墨、水、筆、紙、下敷き、小皿、すずり

＜描く前の準備＞

最初に、濃い墨と薄い墨を作ります。すずりに水を少し入れて、濃い墨をすります。薄い墨は、小皿に入れた水に濃い墨を混ぜて作ります。濃さを見ながら、墨や水の量を調整します。

＜竹の描き方＞

1. 墨を筆に付ける

まず、筆全体に薄い墨を付けます。次に、筆の先に濃い墨を付けます。この薄い墨と濃い墨のバランスによって、きれいにグラデーションを作ることができます。

2. 一本目の竹の幹を描く

紙を押さえながら、筆を横に倒して、下から上に竹の幹を描きます。ゆっくり描くとにじむので、コツは筆を速く動かすことです。節のところで筆を止めながら、竹を描きます。

3. 二本目の竹の幹を描く

二本目は、竹を少し曲げて描きます。筆を横に倒しながら、幹がかすれるように描きます。コツは筆を速く動かすことです。

4. 葉を描く

筆の先を整えながら、筆を立てて、速く描きます。濃い墨の葉と薄い墨の葉をバランスよく混ぜると、竹がきれいに見えます。

5. 枝を描く

節から枝を描きます。細い筆を使うときれいに描けます。節で筆を止めながら、描きます。

6. 節を描く

枝を描き終わったら、節を描きます。コツは紙を押さえながら、節のところに線を描きます。

作品をよくするコツは、墨で絵を描きながら、「余白の美」も考えることです。

1) What are the characteristics of *Sumie*?

2) What do we need to prepare for *Sumie*?

3) What is the process of drawing bamboo?

1.

2.

3.

4.

5.

6.

4) What is one important technique when you draw *Sumie*?

ことばリスト

□墨 □濃淡 □部分 □余白 □空間 □美 □道具 □筆 □下敷き □小皿 □すずり □準備
□薄い □(墨を)する □混ぜる □濃さ □量 □調整する □竹 □(墨を)付ける □(筆の)先
□幹 □(紙を)押さえる □(筆を)倒す □(線が)にじむ □コツ □動かす □(筆を)止める
□曲げる □(線が)かすれる □葉 □(筆を)整える □(筆を)立てる □枝 □節 □線

2 マッチング Matching

Match the keywords and pictures or descriptions below.

ステップ1

例) A

ステップ2

1) ________

ステップ3

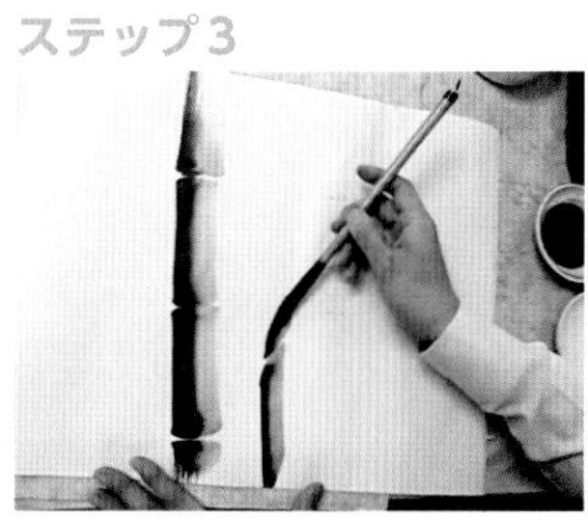

2) ________

ステップ4

3) ________

ステップ5

4) ________

ステップ6

5) ________

A. 筆に墨を付ける。
B. 筆の先を整えながら、葉を描く。
C. 節で筆を止めながら、枝を描く。
D. 紙を押さえながら、節を描く。
E. 紙を押さえながら、竹の幹を描く。
F. 筆を倒しながら、二本目の竹の幹を描く。

Activity 4 ペアでシェアしよう Pair Share

Share your understanding from the previous activities with your partner.

例) まず、筆に墨を付けます。次に、紙を押さえながら、竹の幹を描きます。

Activity 5 グループでシェアしよう Group Share

Converse with your group members about the topic in Japanese.

例) まず、筆に墨を付けます。次に、紙を押さえながら、竹の幹を描きます。

Activity 6
質問に答えよう Respond to the Questions

Answer the following questions based on what you have read about the topic.

例) 竹の幹は、どのように描きますか。
紙を押さえながら、筆を横に倒して、下から上に描きます。

1) 竹の節は、どのように描きますか。

2) 竹の葉は、どのように描きますか。

3) 竹の枝は、どのように描きますか。

4) 作品をよくするコツは何ですか。

3 アイデアを交換しよう Communicate Ideas

Activity 7
文法パターンを見つけよう Let's Explore Language Structure!

1 聞いてみよう Let's Listen!

PPT

Listen to Sensei's presentation and jot down key ideas.

2 新しい文法パターンは？ Where is a New Language Structure?

What is the common language structure? Highlight below.

- 紙を押さえながら、筆を横に倒して、下から上に竹の幹を描きます。
- 筆を横に倒しながら、幹がかすれるように描きます。
- 作品をよくするコツは、墨で絵を描きながら、「余白の美」も考えることです。

3 意味は？ What Could It Mean?

Discuss possible meanings of the language structure as a class.

4 使い方は？ How Can We Use It?

Discuss possible ways to use the language structure as a class.

5 使ってみよう Let's Use the New Language Structure!

Use the language structure in new situations.

例）お母さんは、コーヒーを飲みながらメールをチェックしています。

1) ....

2) ....

3) ....

Activity 8 書いてみよう Write It Out

Express your ideas in writing using the new language structure. List 3 key points when you draw *Sumie.*

私の意見：墨絵を描くときのコツ

1.
2.
3.

Activity 9
ペアでシェアしよう Pair Share

Share your ideas with your partner using the writings from the previous activity.

例) A: 墨絵を描くときのコツは、何ですか。
B: 紙を押さえながら、筆を横に倒して描くことです。

________さんの意見：墨絵を描くときのコツ

1.
2.
3.

Activity 10
まとめてみよう Organize Discussion

Organize your discussion with your partner in Japanese.

Activity 11 ディスカッションしよう Group Discussion

Discuss the topic in groups in Japanese. Use the graphic organizer to capture members' ideas, opinions, and feelings. As you listen to members' ideas, jot down key information in the graphic organizer. Finally, write down the commonalities in the middle section.

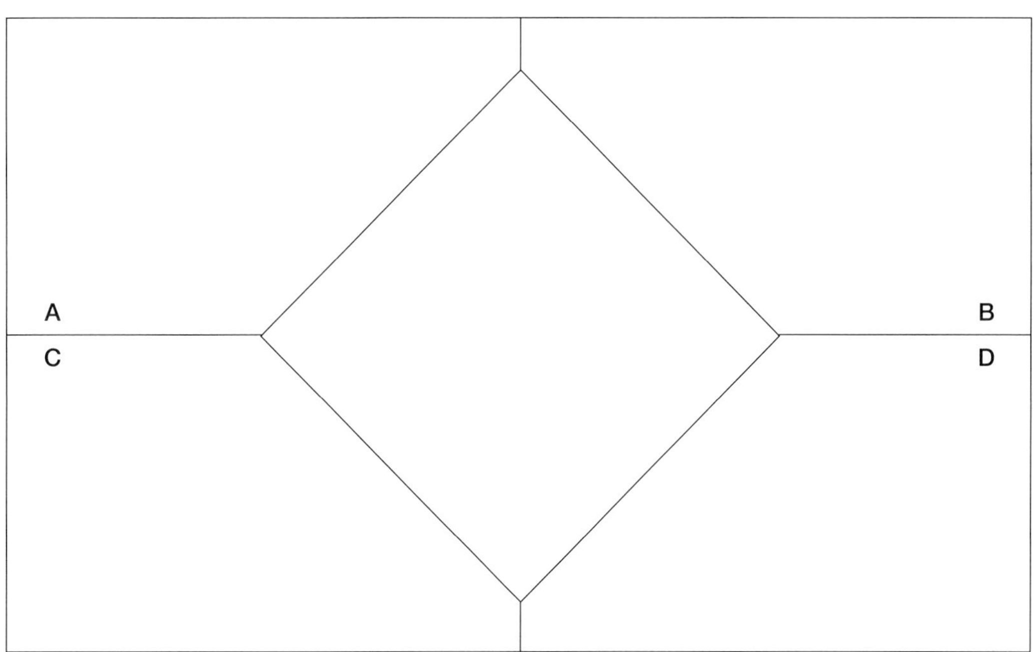

Activity 12 すらすら読もう Read Fluently

Read the article (Activity 3) to your partner. Pay attention to pronunciation, intonation, and tempo as you read aloud.

Activity 13 要約しよう Let's Summarize!

Summarize the article(s) in Japanese.

4 日本語でやってみよう Let's Show What We Can Do!

1 私(わたし)の墨絵(すみえ)

Explanation on My *Sumie* Process (Reflection)

Now that you learned about the concept and process of *Sumie*. You are going to experience *Sumie* drawing. Draw bamboos in *Sumi* ink. Follow each step that you learned in this cycle. After your work is done, share and describe your process for making your piece.

2 墨絵(すみえ)のススメ

Vlog on *Sumie* Experience (Recommendation)

In this learning cycle, you learned about the beauty and process of creating *Sumie*, and experienced creating one of your own. Create a vlog describing your experience creating *Sumie*. Explain the cultural perspectives and steps you took to create your piece. Then, describe how you felt about the experience and recommend *Sumie* to Japanese teenagers. Be detailed and organized by using transitional phrases.

Required

- ☐ ～ながら、～
- ☐ まず／最初(さいしょ)に、～
- ☐ 次(つぎ)に、～
- ☐ 最後(さいご)に、～

Optional

- ☐ なぜなら／その理由(りゆう)は、～からです。
- ☐ また／さらに、～
- ☐ ～と思(おも)います。

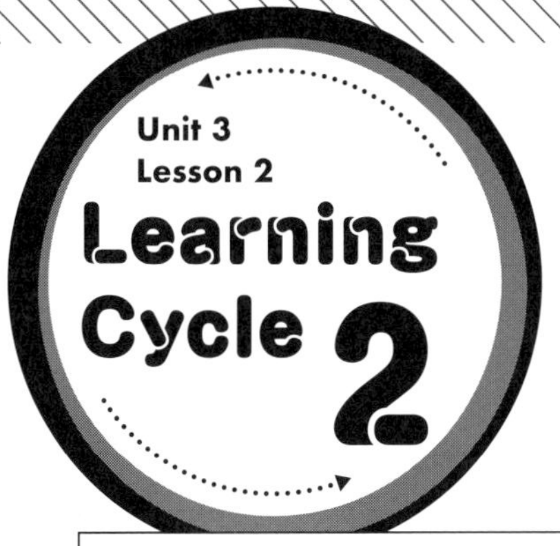

茶道(さどう)の心得(こころえ)

Mindset of *Sado*

What is the philosophy of Sado? In this learning cycle, first you will learn about *Sado*. Then, you will explore the concept behind *Ochakai*. Finally, you will write an article in which you compare *Sado* to a performing art from your country.

0 考えてみよう Let's Explore!

1 What ideas come to your mind when you think about the topic? Jot down keywords in Japanese below.

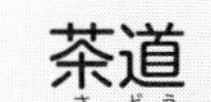

2 Have you heard of the concept of "道(どう)"? Think of other types of "道(どう)" you have heard about in Japanese culture. What do you think is the philosophy behind it?

1 探ってみよう Investigate the World

文化の窓 Take a Look into Japanese Culture

Listen to Sensei's presentation twice. First, take notes on general ideas in English. When you listen a second time, jot down keywords in Japanese.

茶道の心得 Mindset of *Sado*

What is this information about?	
Keywords in Japanese	

まとめてみよう Graphic Organizer

Demonstrate your understanding of the previous presentation by organizing your ideas below.

2 いろいろな視点を学ぼう Recognize Diverse Perspectives

読んで学ぼう Read and Learn

1 読んでみよう Let's Read!

Read and annotate the article below. Then, answer the following comprehension questions.

茶道の心得 Mindset of *Sado*

茶道の茶会は、日本の伝統的な儀式の一つです。「亭主」と呼ばれるホストが、「茶室」と呼ばれる部屋で、客のためにお茶を点てて、もてなします。今の伝統的な茶道の作法（ルール）や茶室を作った人が、千利休です。

では、伝統的な茶会を見てみましょう。茶室の外は「露地」という庭になっています。客はそこにある長椅子に座って、茶会が始まるのを待ちます。茶室はとても神聖な場所ですから、そこで心を落ち着かせなければなりません。そして、茶室に入る前に「つくばい」という水の入った鉢で手を洗って、体を清めなければなりません。

茶室に入るときは、「にじり口」という狭くて小さな入り口から入らなければなりません。入り口の大きさは、高さ約66cm、幅約63cmです。茶室の中もとても狭くて、畳4枚半ぐらいしかありません。どうしてこんなに小さいのでしょうか。千利休は、茶室を身分に関係ない平和で平等な空間にすることを考えました。入り口が小さければ、武士は刀を外に置いて、茶室に入らなければなりません。そして、部屋の中が狭いので、人との距離が近くなります。茶道の茶会では、参加するすべての人が、平等にその空間を楽しみ、その出会いに感謝するのです。

千利休（1522年-1591年）

1) What is *Sado*?

2) What do guests need to do before entering *Chashitsu*?

3) What are some reasons for the size of a *Chashitsu?*

つくばい

にじり口

茶室の中

ことばリスト

□心得 □伝統的 □儀式 □(お茶を)点てる □もてなす □作法 □長椅子 □神聖
□(心を)落ち着かせる □鉢 □(体を)清める □狭い □約～ □幅 □畳 □身分 □関係ない
□平和 □平等 □刀 □距離 □参加する □出会い □感謝する

2 正しい？間違い？ True and False

Read the statements. Write true (○) or false (×) accordingly.

例) 茶会では、客によってお茶が点てられる。	×
1) 茶会では、亭主がもてなされる。	
2) 千利休によって茶道の作法が作られた。	
3) 客は茶室の中の長椅子に座って、心を落ち着かせなければならない。	
4) 客は茶室に入る前に、「にじり口」で手を清めなければならない。	
5) 昔、武士は刀を外に置いて、茶室に入らなければならなかった。	
6) 茶会では、すべての人が平等に楽しみ、出会いに感謝する。	

Activity 4 ペアでシェアしよう Pair Share

Share your understanding from the previous activities with your partner.

例) 茶会では、客は茶室に入る前に「つくばい」で手を清めなければなりません。

Activity 5 グループでシェアしよう Group Share

Converse with your group members about the topic in Japanese.

例) 茶会では、客は茶室に入る前に「つくばい」で手を清めなければなりません。

Activity 6
質問に答えよう Respond to the Questions

Answer the following questions based on what you have read about the topic.

茶道の茶会の作法を教えてください。

例) 客は茶室に入る前に庭にある長椅子に座って、心を落ち着かせなければなりません。

1) ......

2) ......

3) ......

3 アイデアを交換しよう Communicate Ideas

Activity 7
文法パターンを見つけよう Let's Explore Language Structure!

1 聞いてみよう Let's Listen!

PPT

Listen to Sensei's presentation and jot down key ideas.

2 新しい文法パターンは？ Where is a New Language Structure?

What is the common language structure? Highlight below.

- 茶室に入る前に、長椅子に座って心を落ち着かせなければなりません。
- 茶室に入る前に、「つくばい」で体を清めなければなりません。
- 茶室に入るときは、狭くて小さな入り口から入らなければなりません。

3 意味は？ What Could It Mean?

Discuss possible meanings of the language structure as a class.

4 使い方は？ How Can We Use It?

Discuss possible ways to use the language structure as a class.

5 使ってみよう Let's Use the New Language Structure!

Use the language structure in new situations.

例)（レポートの締め切りは明日です！）

➡ 明日までにレポートを出さなければなりません。

1)（明日、大切な試験があります！）

➡

2)（明日、パーティーがあります！）

➡

3)（夏休みに日本へ行きたいです！）

➡

Activity 8 書いてみよう Write It Out

Express your ideas in writing using the new language structure.

私のレポート：茶道の茶会について

茶会とは？
茶会の作法
大切なこと

Activity 9

ペアでシェアしよう Pair Share

Share your ideas with your partner using the writings from the previous activity.

例) A: 茶道の茶会の作法を教えてください。

B: 客は茶室に入る前に、「つくばい」で体を清めなければなりません。

______さんのレポート：茶道の茶会について

茶会とは？
茶会の作法
大切なこと

Activity 10

まとめてみよう Organize Discussion

Organize your discussion with your partner in Japanese.

Activity 11 ディスカッションしよう Group Discussion

Discuss the topic in groups in Japanese. Use the graphic organizer to capture members' ideas, opinions, and feelings. As you listen to members' ideas, jot down key information in the graphic organizer. Finally, write down the commonalities in the middle section.

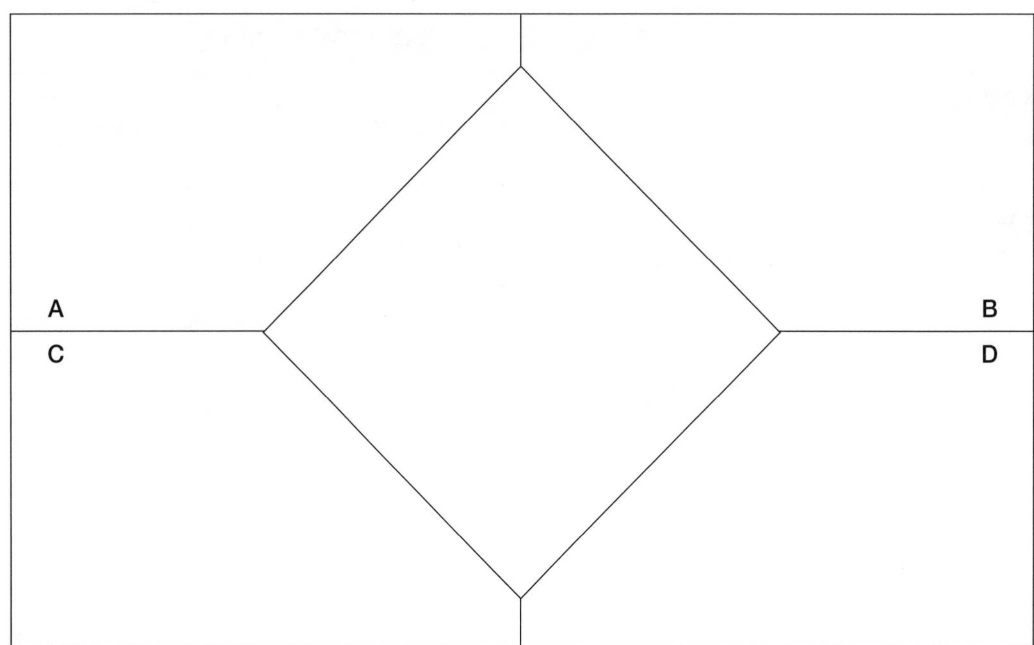

Activity 12 すらすら読もう Read Fluently

Read the article (Activity 3) to your partner. Pay attention to pronunciation, intonation, and tempo as you read aloud.

Activity 13 要約しよう Let's Summarize!

Summarize the article(s) in Japanese.

4 日本語でやってみよう Let's Show What We Can Do!

茶道と私の国の芸術

Sado and My Country's Performing Arts (Comparative Report)

You have explored the concept behind *Ochakai*. Write an article for a Japanese art blog about your opinion on *Sado* and a popular performing art form from your country. Give at least three similarities/differences, and elaborate by providing examples. Lastly, state your preference between the two, and give your reasoning. Incorporate the following structures:

Required

- ☐ ～なければなりません。
- ☐ ～と～を比べてみます。
- ☐ ～に比べて、～

Optional

- ☐ 一方で、～
- ☐ なぜなら／その理由は、～からです。
- ☐ 私の意見としては、～
- ☐ ～と思います。

日本の茶道と＿＿＿＿＿＿

Unit 3 Final Task

日本語でアクション！

Take Action in Japanese!

日本(にほん)と私(わたし) Japan and Me

Task Sheet & Rubrics 

Design and create a piece of artwork to express the relationship between Japan and yourself. You may choose any form of art you have studied in this unit. Your work must reflect your understanding of Japanese culture, sense of beauty, and aesthetics, as well as your personal connection to Japan. Give an online oral presentation to your Japanese exchange school(s).

Salinas Union High School District Japanese Program

Your Role & Purpose	Artists who express their ideas, feelings, etc.
Your Audience	Japanese people
Language	☐ Describe the style of art ☐ Explain each step of your work (e.g., color, tools etc.) ☐ Explain the meaning and influence behind your work ☐ Address its statement, characteristics, and feelings
Product	**Product Type:** Poster/pamphlet/slideshow and your artwork ☐ Hand-drawn or digital ☐ Written description of artwork ☐ Presentation (e.g., online gallery walk)

Unit 4 成功を夢見て
Dream of Success

What does it mean to be an immigrant in a new country?

Lesson 1 歴史から学ぶ移民事情
Learning Immigration Issues from History

Essential Questions:

- How does our history inform us about our current society?
- What did immigrants' lives look like in the past?
- Can love go beyond borders?

Can-do List

Check!

- ☐ Describe major events in the history of Japanese immigrants and Japanese Americans
- ☐ Identify the struggles Japanese immigrants and Japanese Americans faced
- ☐ Describe life experiences that Japanese immigrants and Japanese Americans had been through

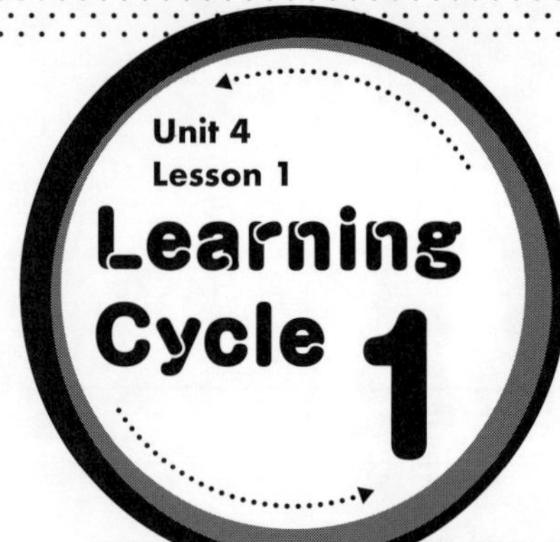

日本人移民の歴史：アメリカ

にほんじんいみん　れきし

History of Japanese Immigrants: The U.S.

How does our history inform us about our current society? In this learning cycle, first you will gain knowledge of Japanese immigrants' immigration experiences. Then you will discuss the quality of their lives with your classmates. Finally, you will report a significant historical event, and state your own opinion in your own words.

0 考えてみよう Let's Explore!

What do you notice in the title picture? (p.133) What ideas come to your mind when you think about the topic? Jot down keywords in Japanese below.

移民（いみん）

1 探ってみよう Investigate the World

文化の窓（ぶんかのまど） Take a Look into Japanese Culture

Listen to Sensei's presentation twice. First, take notes on general ideas in English. When you listen a second time, jot down keywords in Japanese.

日本人移民の歴史：アメリカ　History of Japanese Immigrants: The U.S.

What is this information about?	
Keywords in Japanese	

Activity 2 まとめてみよう　Graphic Organizer

Demonstrate your understanding of the previous presentation by organizing your ideas below.

2 いろいろな視点を学ぼう　Recognize Diverse Perspectives

Activity 3 読んで学ぼう　Read and Learn

1 読んでみよう　Let's Read!

Read and annotate the article below. Then, answer the following comprehension questions.

日本人移民の歴史：アメリカ　History of Japanese Immigrants: The U.S.　13

日本人が海外に移住した背景：日本では1860年以降、人口が急に増え、特に農村では土地も仕事もない人々が多く、大きな問題になっていた。そのため、日本政府は移民政策を積極的に進めた。そして、多くの人々が仕事を求めて、海外へ移住していった。アメリカへの移住は、グアム島、ハワイ、カリフォルニアから始まった。

1) Why did Japanese people immigrate from the 1860s?

1868年：約150人の日本人が初めてハワイに移住した。

1905年：サンフランシスコで反日運動*が始まった。次の年、日本人移民の子どもは別の学校に行かされた。

1924年：新しい移民法*により、日本からアメリカへの移民が禁止された。

1941年12月：真珠湾攻撃*の後、太平洋戦争*が始まった。

1942年-1946年：日本人移民と日系アメリカ人は強制収容所*に行かされ、大変な生活をさせられた。

1945年8月：広島と長崎に原爆が落とされた。日本はポツダム宣言*を認めさせられ、第二次世界大戦*は終わった。

1952年：マッカラン・ウォルター法（移民国籍法）*が成立し、日本人移民に市民権が認められた。

1988年：レーガン大統領*が強制収容について謝罪した。そして、強制収容所でつらい生活をさせられた日本人移民や日系アメリカ人に、2万ドルの賠償金が払われた。

現在の日本人移民と日系アメリカ人：このような経験から、この世界で同じようなことが二度と起きないようにという思いで、さまざまな活動をしている。

* 反日運動 Anti-Japanese movement、移民法 immigration law、真珠湾攻撃 Attack on Pearl Harbor、太平洋戦争 Pacific War、強制収容所 concentration camp、ポツダム宣言 Potsdam Declaration、第二次世界大戦 World War II、マッカラン・ウォルター法（移民国籍法）McCarran-Walter Act、レーガン大統領 President Reagan

2) Where did Japanese people immigrate first in 1868?

3) What happened in 1905 in San Francisco?

4) Immigration from Japan to the U.S. was banned due to...!

5) Where were the Japanese Immigrants and Japanese Americans sent in 1942?

6) What is the purpose of the Japanese Americans' and Japanese immigrants' movements?

ことばリスト

□移民　□歴史　□海外　□移住する　□背景　□～以降　□人口　□急に　□農村　□土地　□政府

□移民政策　□積極的　□(政策を)進める　□(仕事を)求める　□禁止する　□日系　□原爆（＝原子爆弾）

□認める　□(法律が)成立する　□市民権　□謝罪する　□賠償金　□払う　□経験　□二度と（～ない）

□同じようなこと　□起きる

2 マッチング Matching

Match the keywords and pictures or descriptions below.

1868年

例) A

1905年

1) ______

1941年

2) ______

1942年-1946年

3) ______

1945年

4) ______

1952年

5) ______

A. 約150人の日本人が初めてハワイに移住した。
B. 日本人移民と日系アメリカ人は強制収容所に行かされ、大変な生活をさせられた。
C. マッカラン・ウォルター法（移民国籍法）が成立し、日本人移民に市民権が認められた。
D. 日本人移民の子どもは別の学校に行かされた。
E. 日本はポツダム宣言を認めさせられ、第二次世界大戦は終わった。
F. 真珠湾攻撃の後、太平洋戦争が始まった。

Activity 4
ペアでシェアしよう Pair Share

Share your understanding from the previous activities with your partner.

例) 1905年に、サンフランシスコで反日運動が始まって、日本人移民の子どもは別の学校に行かされました。

Activity 5
グループでシェアしよう Group Share

Converse with your group members about the topic in Japanese.

例) 1905年に、サンフランシスコで反日運動が始まって、日本人移民の子どもは別の学校に行かされました。

Activity 6
質問に答えよう Respond to the Questions

Answer the following questions based on what you have read about the topic.

例) 1906年にサンフランシスコでどんなことがありましたか。

日本人移民の子どもは別の学校に行かされました。

1) 1924年にどんなことがありましたか。

2) 1942年から1946年の間にどんなことがありましたか。

3) 1945年8月にどんなことがありましたか。

3 アイデアを交換しよう Communicate Ideas

Activity 7
文法パターンを見つけよう Let's Explore Language Structure!

1 聞いてみよう Let's Listen!

PPT

Listen to Sensei's presentation and jot down key ideas.

2 新しい文法パターンは？ Where is a New Language Structure?

What is the common language structure? Highlight below.

- 日本人移民の子どもは別の学校に行かされた。
- 日本人移民と日系アメリカ人は強制収容所に行かされ、大変な生活をさせられた。
- 日本はポツダム宣言を認めさせられ、第二次世界大戦は終わった。

3 意味は？ What Could It Mean?

Discuss possible meanings of the language structure as a class.

4 使い方は？ How Can We Use It?

Discuss possible ways to use the language structure as a class.

5 使ってみよう Let's Use the New Language Structure!

Use the language structure in new situations.

嫌なことをさせられた経験を教えてください。

例）小さいときに、よく野菜を食べさせられました。

1）

2）

3）

Activity 8 書いてみよう Write It Out

Express your ideas in writing using the new language structure.

私の意見

日本人移民がさせられたこと	どう思う？
1.	
2.	
3.	

Activity 9 ペアでシェアしよう Pair Share

Share your ideas with your partner using the writings from the previous activity.

例) A: 昔、日本人移民は何をさせられましたか。
B: 日本人移民の子どもは、別の学校に行かされました。

＿＿＿＿＿＿さんの意見

日本人移民がさせられたこと	どう思う？
1.	
2.	
3.	

Activity 10 まとめてみよう Organize Discussion

Organize your discussion with your partner in Japanese.

Activity 11
ディスカッションしよう Group Discussion

Discuss the topic in groups in Japanese. Use the graphic organizer to capture members' ideas, opinions, and feelings. As you listen to members' ideas, jot down key information in the graphic organizer. Finally, write down the commonalities in the middle section.

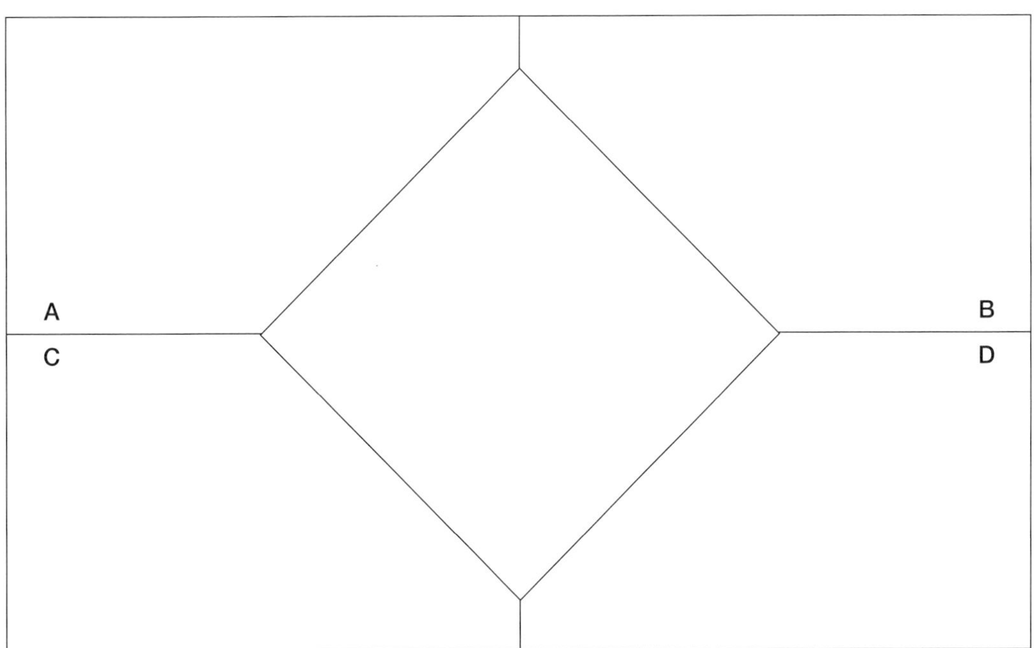

Activity 12
すらすら読もう Read Fluently

Read the article (Activity 3) to your partner. Pay attention to pronunciation, intonation, and tempo as you read aloud.

Activity 13
要約しよう Let's Summarize!

Summarize the article(s) in Japanese.

 日本語でやってみよう Let's Show What We Can Do!

日本人移民の生活 Life of Japanese Immigrants (Presentation)

Japanese students are visiting your classroom. Make a presentation with your partner about Japanese immigrants' history and background information. Choose three significant events and/or experiences. State your opinion on the events. Use phrases from below to help draft your summary.

Required

- □ ～させられました。（Causative-Passive Form）
- □ なぜなら／その理由は、～からです。

Optional

- □ 私の意見では、～
- □ ～と思います。
- □ まず、～
- □ 次に、～
- □ また／さらに、～

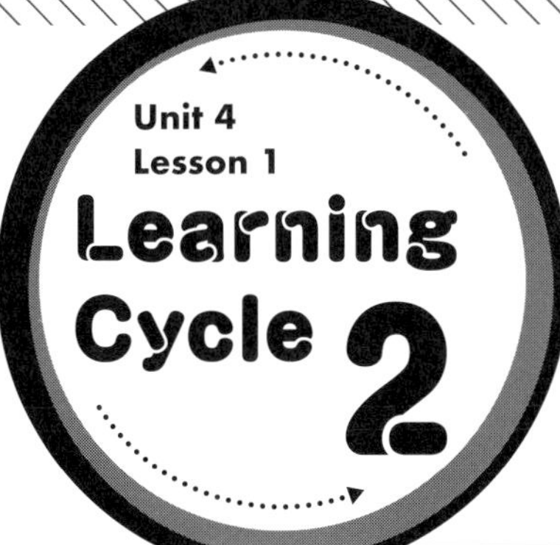

愛は国境を越える

あい　こっきょう　こ

Love Goes Beyond Borders

Can love go beyond borders? In this learning cycle, you will first learn about the story of a Japanese woman and an American man who met after World War II in Japan. Then, you will share your thoughts and feelings about human relationships which exist beyond nationalities. Finally, you will research a person's immigration experience and write a short biography. You will also write a Cinquain to express your thoughts and feelings about moving to another country.

0 考えてみよう Let's Explore!

What ideas come to your mind when you think about the topic? Jot down keywords in Japanese below.

国際結婚
こくさいけっこん

1 探ってみよう Investigate the World

文化の窓 Take a Look into Japanese Culture

ぶんか　まど

Listen to Sensei's presentation twice. First, take notes on general ideas in English. When you listen a second time, jot down keywords in Japanese.

愛は国境を越える　Love Goes Beyond Borders

What is this information about?	
Keywords in Japanese	

Activity 2 まとめてみよう　Graphic Organizer

Demonstrate your understanding of the previous presentation by organizing your ideas below.

2 いろいろな視点を学ぼう　Recognize Diverse Perspectives

Activity 3 読んで学ぼう　Read and Learn

1 読んでみよう　Let's Read!

Read and annotate the article below. Then, answer the following comprehension questions.

愛は国境を越える　Love Goes Beyond Borders

インタビュアー：今日はお忙しい中、ありがとうございます。まず、初子・ジェンキンスさんの生い立ちについて少し教えてください。

ジェンキンス：私は 1931年に、日本の川崎というところで生まれました。私の家族は沖縄の出身なんですが、戦争から

1) Where is Hatsuko originally from?

逃れるため、沖縄から川崎のほうに疎開*して暮らしていました。家族と沖縄に帰ったのは私が16歳のときでした。

インタビュアー：そうですか。沖縄での生活はどうでしたか。

ジェンキンス：戦後の沖縄には何もありませんでした。それでも、沖縄の人は復興のために力を合わせてがんばって生活をしていました。もちろん大変でしたが、活気のある時期でもありました。高校生になった私は、アメリカ軍のカミサリーというスーパーで働いていました。

インタビュアー：そのときにご主人のビル・ジェンキンスさんに出会ったのですか。

ジェンキンス：そうです。やせて背の高い青い目のアメリカ軍人が、いつも微笑んで私に沖縄の方言で話すんですよ。びっくりしましたよ。でも、彼の優しさと人柄にすぐに恋に落ちました。

インタビュアー：ご両親はビルさんと初子さんの関係をどう思っていましたか。

ジェンキンス：最初はとても反対していました。それはそうですよ。ビルは敵だった国の人。15歳も年上。それに、日本語もあまり話せなかったんです。でも、あんなに反対していた両親も彼と会ってからは、私たちのことを認めるようになりました。彼の人柄のおかげでしょうね。

インタビュアー：よかったですね。その後、いつごろアメリカへ移住したのですか。

ジェンキンス：当時のアメリカでは、違う人種の人との結婚はまだ認められていませんでした。でも、なぜか軍人だけはほかの国籍の人との結婚が許されていました。1955年に沖縄で結婚をして、その年にハワイへ移住しました。国際結婚でさまざまな苦労もしましたが、今はとても幸せです。

インタビュアー：まさに愛は国境を越えるんですね。

* 疎開 evacuation

2) Describe life in Okinawa.

3) Where did Hatsuko meet her future husband?

4) What are some characteristics of Bill?

5) What were some presumed obstacles Hatsuko and Bill faced?

6) How did Hatsuko and Bill overcome their challenges?

ことばリスト

□愛　□国境　□(国境を)越える　□生い立ち　□出身　□(戦争から)逃れる　□暮らす　□戦後　□復興
あい　　こっきょう　　こっきょう　こ　　　　　　おいた　　　しゅっしん　　せんそう　　のが　　　　　　　く　　　　　せんご　　ふっこう

□力　□(力を)合わせる　□活気(のある)　□時期　□～軍　□軍人　□微笑む　□方言　□優しさ
ちから　ちから　あ　　　　かっき　　　　　じき　　　ぐん　　ぐんじん　　ほほえ　　ほうげん　　やさ

□人柄　□恋　□(恋に)落ちる　□関係　□反対する　□敵　□当時　□人種　□国籍　□結婚
ひとがら　こい　　こい　お　　　　かんけい　はんたい　　　てき　　とうじ　　じんしゅ　こくせき　けっこん

□(結婚を)許す　□国際結婚　□苦労する　□幸せ
けっこん　ゆる　　こくさいけっこん　　くろう　　　しあわ

2 正しい？間違い？ True and False

Read the statements. Write true (○) or false (×) accordingly.

例) 初子さんは、1931年に沖縄で生まれました。	×
1) 初子さんは、小さいときに川崎で暮らしていました。	
2) 初子さんは、16歳のときに沖縄に帰りました。	
3) 初子さんは、高校生のとき学校で働いていました。	
4) 初子さんは、ビルさんが背が高かったので好きになりました。	
5) 初子さんの両親は、最初ビルさんのことを反対していました。	
6) 初子さんとビルさんは、カリフォルニアに移住しました。	
7) 昔のアメリカでは、違う人種の人との結婚は認められていませんでした。	

Activity 4
ペアでシェアしよう Pair Share

Share your understanding from the previous activities with your partner.

例) 初子さんは、小さいときに川崎で暮らしていました。

Activity 5
グループでシェアしよう Group Share

Converse with your group members about the topic in Japanese.

例) 初子さんは、小さいときに川崎で暮らしていました。

Activity 6
質問に答えよう Respond to the Questions

Answer the following questions based on what you have read about the topic.

例）初子さんは、ハワイに移住する前にどこに住んでいましたか。
沖縄に住んでいました。

1) ビルさんは、沖縄で何をしていましたか。

2) 初子さんは、高校生のとき何をしていましたか。

3) 初子さんの両親は、最初ビルさんと初子さんの関係をどう思っていましたか。

3 アイデアを交換しよう Communicate Ideas

Activity 7
文法パターンを見つけよう Let's Explore Language Structure!

1 聞いてみよう Let's Listen!

PPT

Listen to Sensei's presentation and jot down key ideas.

2 新しい文法パターンは？ Where is a New Language Structure?

What is the common language structure? Highlight below.

- 初子さんの家族は、沖縄から川崎のほうに疎開して暮らしていました。
- 初子さんは、アメリカ軍のカミサリーというスーパーで働いていました。
- 初子さんの両親は、最初はとても反対していました。

3 意味は？ What Could It Mean?

Discuss possible meanings of the language structure as a class.

4 使い方は？ How Can We Use It?

Discuss possible ways to use the language structure as a class.

5 使ってみよう Let's Use the New Language Structure!

Use the language structure in new situations.

例)（小さいとき）

➡ 小さいとき、日本の川崎というところに住んでいました。

1)（小さいとき）

➡

2)（中学生のとき）

➡

3)（高校に入ったとき）

➡

Activity 8 書いてみよう Write It Out

Express your ideas in writing using the new language structure.

私の家族

生まれた町はどこ？	
今はどこに住んでいる？	
引っ越した経験がある？	
小さいとき、どんな生活をしていた？	
その経験について、どう思っている？	

Activity 9
ペアでシェアしよう Pair Share

Share your ideas with your partner using the writings from the previous activity.

例) A: 生まれた町はどこですか。
B: カリフォルニアのロサンゼルスで生まれました。

____________さんの家族

生まれた町はどこ？	
今はどこに住んでいる？	
引っ越した経験がある？	
小さいとき、どんな生活をしていた？	
その経験について、どう思っている？	

Activity 10
まとめてみよう Organize Discussion

Organize your discussion with your partner in Japanese.

Activity 11
ディスカッションしよう　Group Discussion

Discuss the topic in groups in Japanese. Use the graphic organizer to capture members' ideas, opinions, and feelings. As you listen to members' ideas, jot down key information in the graphic organizer. Finally, write down the commonalities in the middle section.

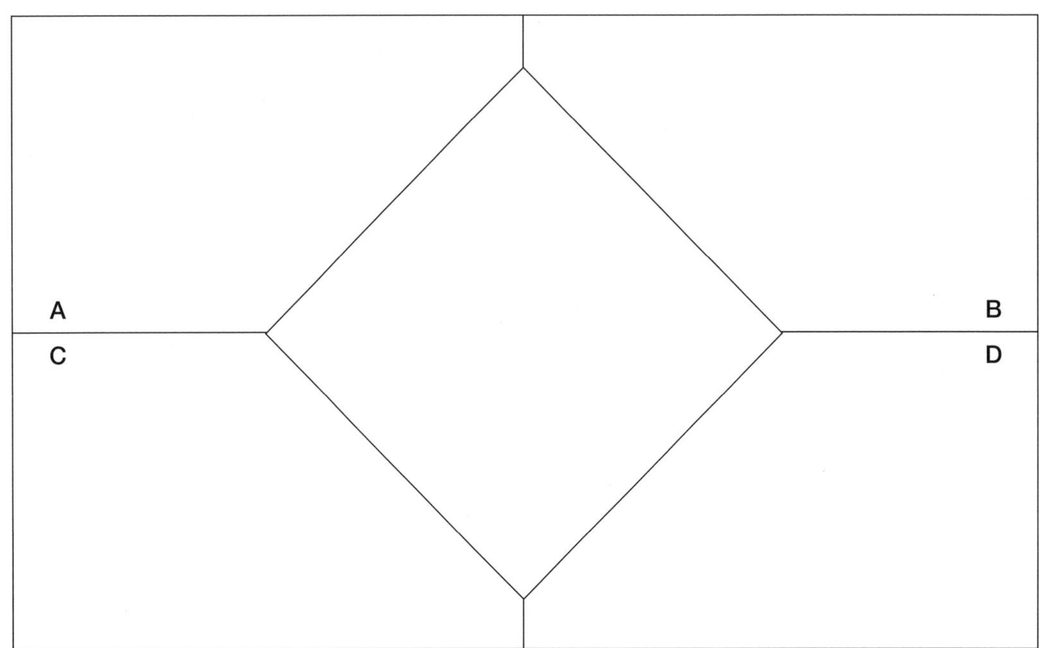

Activity 12
すらすら読(よ)もう　Read Fluently

Read the article (Activity 3) to your partner. Pay attention to pronunciation, intonation, and tempo as you read aloud.

Activity 13
要約(ようやく)しよう　Let's Summarize!

Summarize the article(s) in Japanese.

4 日本語でやってみよう Let's Show What We Can Do!

移民の生活 An Immigrant's Life (Biography)

You have learned about the human relationships that exist beyond nationalities. In order to spread the knowldge more about immigration stories for Japanese high school students, interview someone who has immigrated to your country. Find out the reasons for starting a new life in another country and the experiences they have faced. Finally, compile your interview in a short biography in Japanese so Japanese readers can learn from your interviewee's valuable life experiences.

Required

☐ ～ていました。
☐ ～ています。
☐ ～とき、～

Optional

☐ ～そうです。

日本語でアクション!

Take Action in Japanese!

移民について Immigration Experience (Cinquain)

Now you have gained insights of people's immigration experiences through stories. You are invited to enter your poem to a contest of a Japanese newspaper. Express your thoughts and feelings in Japanese using the Cinquain form.

What is a Cinquain?

A Cinquain is a short and striking or memorable phrase used in advertising. Write a Cinquain based on the interview from the previous autobiography task. You may add a picture to enhance the emotional impact of your Cinquain.

Line A: One word (Subject of Cinquain)

....

Line B: Two words (adjectives to describe the subject)

....

Line C: Three action words

....

Line D: Four-word phrase (feeling about the subject)

....

Line E: One word (Synonym for the subject)

....

異国

新しい　違う

夢を見る　働く　学ぶ

家族と将来のためにがんばる

移民

新しい国

ワクワク　どきどき

恋に落ちる　結婚する　暮らす

将来の期待と不安を乗り越えて

アメリカ

Unit 4 成功を夢見て Dream of Success

What does it mean to be an immigrant in a new country?

Lesson 2 現代の移民事情 Current Immigration Issues

Essential Questions:

- What motivates people to consider moving to a new country?
- What defines being successful in another country?
- What does the life of immigrants look like in a new country?

Can-do Lost

- ☐ Identify and describe the reasons for immigration
- ☐ Discuss life events, struggles, and conflicts among family members
- ☐ Narrate family immigration story

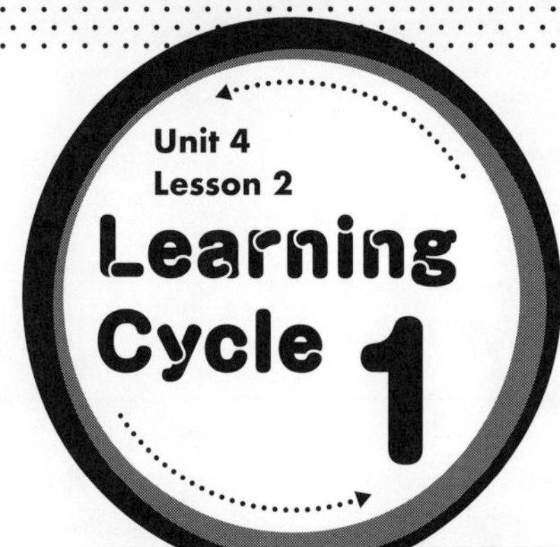

移民の国：アメリカ

Country of Immigration: The U.S.

Moving to a new country is a major life event. What motivates people to consider moving to a new country? In this learning cycle, first, you will explore the purpose for people immigrating to the U.S. Then, you will discuss your opinions and feelings towards immigration with your classmates. Finally, give a presentation about the major reasons for immigration and your thoughts about them.

0 考えてみよう Let's Explore!

What do you notice in the title picture? (p.153) What ideas come to your mind when you think about the topic? Jot down keywords in Japanese below.

移民する理由

1 探ってみよう Investigate the World

Activity 1 文化の窓 Take a Look into Japanese Culture

Listen to Sensei's presentation twice. First, take notes on general ideas in English. When you listen a second time, jot down keywords in Japanese.

移民の国：アメリカ Country of Immigration: The U.S.

What is this information about?	
Keywords in Japanese	

Activity 2 まとめてみよう Graphic Organizer

Demonstrate your understanding of the previous presentation by organizing your ideas below.

2 いろいろな視点を学ぼう Recognize Diverse Perspectives

Activity 3 読んで学ぼう Read and Learn

1 読んでみよう Let's Read!

Read and annotate the article below. Then, answer the following comprehension questions.

移民の国：アメリカ Country of Immigration: The U.S.

もともとアメリカには、ネイティブ・アメリカン*と呼ばれる先住民が住んでいました。17世紀の初め、宗教の自由を求めて、イギリス人がアメリカに来ました。その後、北ヨーロッパや西ヨーロッパから、同じように宗教の自由を求めて、多くの人がアメリカに移住しました。

19世紀の半ばごろ、飢餓や貧困から逃れるために、100万人以上の人がアイルランドからアメリカに来ました。19世紀の終わりごろから、イタリアなど南ヨーロッパの人々が貧困から逃れるために、そして、ロシアなどからユダヤ人が迫害から逃れるためにアメリカに来ました。

20世紀以降も、貧困や戦争から逃れて、自由や平等を求めて、メキシコ、中南米、中近東、アジアなどからも多くの人がアメリカに移住しています。

現在、アメリカには5000万人を超える移民が住んでいます。今でも世界中から毎年100万人近い人が、豊かな生活を求めて、アメリカにチャンスをつかみに来ます。アメリカに、いい教育を受けに来たり、いい仕事を探しに来たりする人がたくさんいるのです。

アメリカン・ドリームとは、自由と平等の権利のもとに、だれでも夢をかなえるチャンスがあるという考えのことです。例えば、カリフォルニア州のシリコンバレー*には、有名なIT企業がたくさんあって、そのCEOやエンジニアの多くは移民です。彼らはチャンスと成功を夢見て、アメリカに働きに来ました。そして、アメリカン・ドリームをかなえたのです。

* **ネイティブ・アメリカン** Native Americans、**シリコンバレー** Silicon Valley

1) Why did people immigrate during the following period?

-17 century

-19 century

-20 century

-recent

2) What is the "American Dream" defined in this article?

3) What is an example of immigrant success?

4) What are some similarities among people who seek to immigrate to the U.S.?

ことばリスト

□もともと □先住民 □宗教 □自由 □半ば □飢餓 □貧困 □迫害 □戦争 □中南米 □中近東

□(~万人を)超える □世界中 □豊かな □(チャンスを)つかむ □教育 □(教育)を受ける □権利

□(夢を)かなえる □~州 □企業 □成功 □夢見る

2 正しい？間違い？ True and False

Read the statements. Write true (○) or false (×) accordingly.

例）多くの人がアメリカに家族に会いに来る。	×
1) 多くの人がアメリカにチャンスをつかみに来る。	
2) 多くの人がアメリカにいい教育を受けに来る。	
3) 多くの人がアメリカにお金をもらいに来る。	
4) 多くの人がアメリカに働きに来る。	
5) 多くの人がアメリカに日本語を勉強しに来る。	
6) 多くの人がアメリカにいい仕事を探しに来る。	
7) 多くの人がアメリカに夢をかなえに来る。	

Activity 4 ペアでシェアしよう Pair Share

Share your understanding from the previous activities with your partner.

例）多くの人がアメリカにチャンスをつかみに来ます。

Activity 5 グループでシェアしよう Group Share

Converse with your group members about the topic in Japanese.

例）多くの人がアメリカにチャンスをつかみに来ます。

Activity 6
質問に答えよう　Respond to the Questions

Answer the following questions based on what you have read about the topic.

世界中から毎年100万人近い人が、アメリカに何をしに来ますか。

例）豊かな生活を求めて、チャンスをつかみに来ます。

1）

2）

3）

3 アイデアを交換しよう　Communicate Ideas

Activity 7
文法パターンを見つけよう　Let's Explore Language Structure!

1 聞いてみよう　Let's Listen!

PPT

Listen to Sensei's presentation and jot down key ideas.

2 新しい文法パターンは？　Where is a New Language Structure?

What is the common language structure? Highlight below.

- 今でも世界中から毎年100万人近い人が、豊かな生活を求めて、アメリカにチャンスをつかみに来ます。
- アメリカに、いい教育を受けに来たり、いい仕事を探しに来たりする人がたくさんいるのです。
- 彼らはチャンスと成功を夢見て、アメリカに働きに来ました。

3 意味は？　What Could It Mean?

Discuss possible meanings of the language structure as a class.

4 使い方は？ How Can We Use It?

Discuss possible ways to use the language structure as a class.

5 使ってみよう Let's Use the New Language Structure!

Use the language structure in new situations.

例) 日本に行く理由は何ですか。
おいしいものを食べに行きます。

1) 日本に行く理由は何ですか。

2) 大学に行く理由は何ですか。

3) ______________ 理由は何ですか。

Activity 8 書いてみよう Write It Out

Express your ideas in writing using the new language structure.

私の意見：人々が新しい国に移民する理由

1.
2.
3.

Activity 9

ペアでシェアしよう Pair Share

Share your ideas with your partner using the writings from the previous activity.

例) A: 人々は、新しい国に何をしに行きますか。
B: いい教育を受けに行きます。

______さんの意見：人々が新しい国に移民する理由

1.
2.
3.

Activity 10

まとめてみよう Organize Discussion

Organize your discussion with your partner in Japanese.

Activity 11
ディスカッションしよう　Group Discussion

Discuss the topic in groups in Japanese. Use the graphic organizer to capture members' ideas, opinions, and feelings. As you listen to members' ideas, jot down key information in the graphic organizer. Finally, write down the commonalities in the middle section.

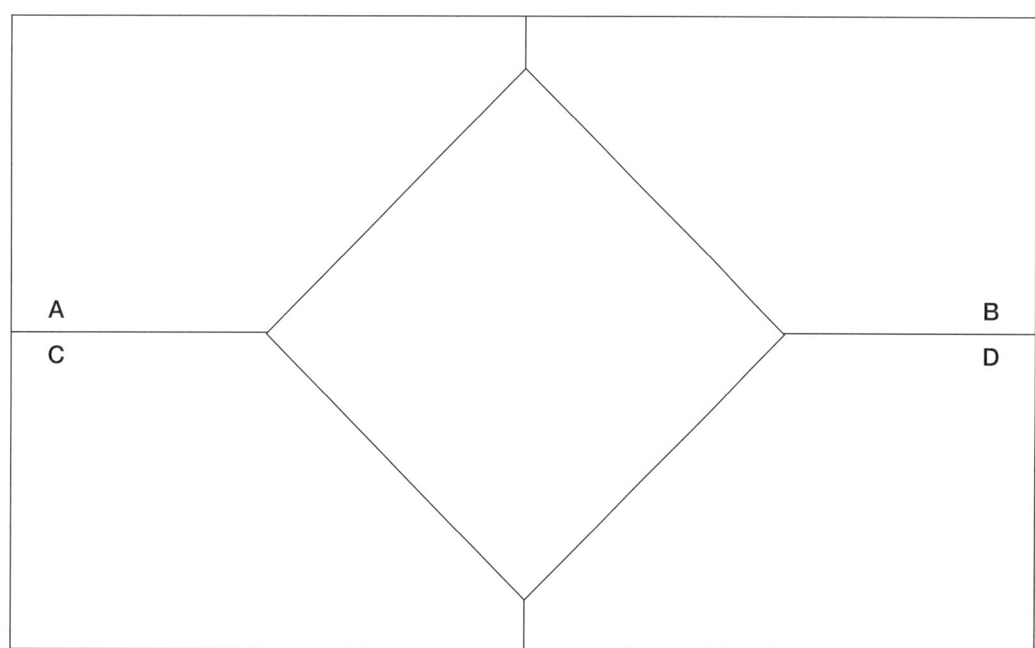

Activity 12
すらすら読(よ)もう　Read Fluently

Read the article (Activity 3) to your partner. Pay attention to pronunciation, intonation, and tempo as you read aloud.

Activity 13
要約(ようやく)しよう　Let's Summarize!

Summarize the article(s) in Japanese.

日本語でやってみよう Let's Show What We Can Do!

移民する理由 Reasons for Immigration (Presentation)

You are hosting an online presentation to Japanese high school students about immigration trends in your country Describe three major purposes of people immigrating to your country Finally, state your opinion and feelings towards such reasons. You may use phrases from below to help draft your summary.

Required

□【Purpose】に来ます／行きます。

Optional

□ ～させられました。
（Causative-Passive Form）

□ ～ていました／ています。

□ なぜなら／その理由は、～からです。

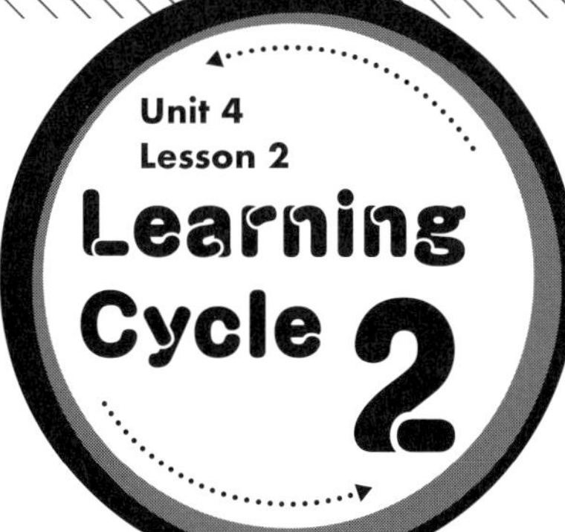

私の家族の移民物語
わたし　かぞく　いみんものがたり

My Family's Immigration Stories

What does the life of immigrants look like in a new country? In this learning cycle, first, you will learn about one immigrant family's experience. Then, you will share your own family story and share common experiences with classmates. Lastly, you will write your family immigration story to be included in a collection of "Our American Stories."

0 考えてみよう Let's Explore!

What ideas come to your mind when you think about the topic? Jot down keywords in Japanese below.

アメリカン
ドリーム

1 探ってみよう Investigate the World

文化の窓 Take a Look into Japanese Culture
ぶんか　まど

Listen to Sensei's presentation twice. First, take notes on general ideas in English. When you listen a second time, jot down keywords in Japanese.

私の家族の移民物語 My Family's Immigration Stories

What is this information about?	
Keywords in Japanese	

Activity 2
まとめてみよう Graphic Organizer

Demonstrate your understanding of the previous presentation by organizing your ideas below.

2 いろいろな視点を学ぼう Recognize Diverse Perspectives

Activity 3
読んで学ぼう Read and Learn

1 読んでみよう Let's Read!

Read and annotate the article below. Then, answer the following comprehension questions.

私の家族の移民物語 My Family's Immigration Stories

私の名前はブランドン・ヌエンです。父はベトナム人、母はメキシコ人です。両親はそれぞれ十代のときにアメリカに移住したそうです。

父の移民の経験

正直言って、私は父の移民の話をあまりよく知りません。知りたくても、父はあまり話したがりません。ベトナムでつらい経験をいろいろしたのだと思います。私が知っているこ

1) Why did the father leave his country?

2) How old was the father when he came to the U.S.?

とは、ベトナム戦争中にアメリカに移住したということです。食料が少なくて、生活が大変で、家族を残して一人で難民として海を渡ったそうです。十代でアメリカに来た父は、安定した生活ができるようにいろいろな仕事をしました。そのため、父は教育を受けたくても、受けられませんでした。やがて、父は美容師になりました。美容師の仕事のおかげで、母に出会ったそうです。母も美容師でした。そして、結婚して、6人の子どもを育てました。その一人が私です。

母の移民の経験

私の母は自分の移民の話をよくします。母は幼いころに、メキシコの田舎に住んでいました。その時、祖父は大けがをして、仕事がしたくてもできませんでした。仕事を休んでいる間、祖父はアメリカに移住したい気持ちが強くなったそうです。最初に祖父が一人でアメリカに移住しました。そして、カリフォルニア州の農場で仕事をしました。その後、残りの家族全員がアメリカに移住しました。母によると、国境にある川を渡って、カリフォルニア州に来たそうです。そのころ、母は中学生ぐらいでした。母は兄弟の中で一番年上でした。日本にも同じ考え方があると思いますが、メキシコにも、年長の子どもは特別な責任があります。例えば、兄弟の世話をしなければなりません。母は学校に行きたくても、家族を助けるために農場で働きました。でも、二十歳になったときに、美容師の仕事を始めました。そこで父に出会ったそうです。

つらくても、お互いに支え合って、家族のためにがんばっている両親に感謝しています。だから、私もがんばります。

Yo Azama『Our American Stories (Volume 1) (Japanese Edition)』より

3) Why couldn't the father receive an education in the U.S.?

4) What kind of job did the mother's father do when he came to the U.S.?

5) How did the entire family move from Mexico to the U.S.?

6) What is the responsibility of the oldest child in Mexican families?

7) How does the author feel about his parents' immigration?

ことばリスト 

□両親 □それぞれ □正直 □食料 □(家族を)残す □難民 □(海／川を)渡る □安定する
□やがて □美容師 □出会う □育てる □幼い □田舎 □祖父 □大けが(をする) □農場
□年上 □考え方 □年長 □特別 □責任 □世話(をする) □つらい □お互い □支え合う

2 分けてみよう Categorizing

Write the keywords in the appropriate categories.

父	どちらも	母
	A	

A. 十代のとき、アメリカに移住した。

B. あまり自分の移民の話をしない。

C. よく自分の移民の話をする。

D. 川を渡って、アメリカに来た。

E. 家族のために、がんばっている。

F. 6人の子どもを育てている。

G. 難民として一人で海を渡った。

H. つらい経験をした。

I. 学校に行きたくても、家族を助けるために農場で働いた。

J. 仕事のために、教育を受けたくても受けられなかった。

K. お父さんはカリフォルニアの農場で働いていた。

L. 美容師になった。

Activity 4

ペアでシェアしよう Pair Share

Share your understanding from the previous activities with your partner.

例）ブランドンさんが知りたくても、お父さんはあまり自分の移民の話をしません。

Activity 5

グループでシェアしよう Group Share

Converse with your group members about the topic in Japanese.

例）ブランドンさんが知りたくても、お父さんはあまり自分の移民の話をしません。

Activity 6 質問に答えよう Respond to the Questions

Answer the following questions based on what you have read about the topic.

例）ブランドンさんは、お父さんの移民の話を知っていますか。
知りたくても、お父さんはあまり話したがりません。

1）ブランドンさんのお父さんは、教育を受けることができましたか。

2）ブランドンさんのおじいさんは、メキシコで仕事ができましたか。

3）ブランドンさんのお母さんは、学校に行けましたか。

3 アイデアを交換しよう Communicate Ideas

Activity 7 文法パターンを見つけよう Let's Explore Language Structure!

1 聞いてみよう Let's Listen!

Listen to Sensei's presentation and jot down key ideas.

2 新しい文法パターンは？ Where is a New Language Structure?

What is the common language structure? Highlight below.

- 父の移民の話を知りたくても、父はあまり話したがりません。
- 父は教育を受けたくても、受けられませんでした。
- つらくても、お互いに支え合って、家族のためにがんばっている両親に感謝しています。

3 意味は？ What Could It Mean?

Discuss possible meanings of the language structure as a class.

4 使い方は？ How Can We Use It?

Discuss possible ways to use the language structure as a class.

5 使ってみよう Let's Use the New Language Structure!

Use the language structure in new situations.

例) アルバイトをしたい。でも、時間がない。
➡ アルバイトをしたくても、時間がありません。

1) 大学に行きたい。でも、お金がない。
➡

2) プロのゲーマーになりたい。でも、親に反対される。
➡

3) 難しいことがたくさんある。でも、あきらめない。
➡

Activity 8 書いてみよう Write It Out

Express your ideas in writing using the new language structure.

私の家族／知り合いの移民情報

移民した人と その人との関係	
移民したときと 移民したところ	
つらかったこと	
そのときの気持ち	

Activity 9
ペアでシェアしよう Pair Share

Share your ideas with your partner using the writings from the previous activity.

例) A: 移民した人はだれですか。いつ、どこに移民しましたか。つらかったことは何ですか。

B: 私の祖父です。十代のときメキシコからカリフォルニアに来ました。お金がなくて、教育を受けたくても、受けられませんでした。

＿＿＿＿＿＿さんの家族／知り合いの移民情報

移民した人とその人との関係	
移民したときと移民したところ	
つらかったこと	
そのときの気持ち	

Activity 10
まとめてみよう Organize Discussion

Organize your discussion with your partner in Japanese.

Activity 11 ディスカッションしよう Group Discussion

Discuss the topic in groups in Japanese. Use the graphic organizer to capture members' ideas, opinions, and feelings. As you listen to members' ideas, jot down key information in the graphic organizer. Finally, write down the commonalities in the middle section.

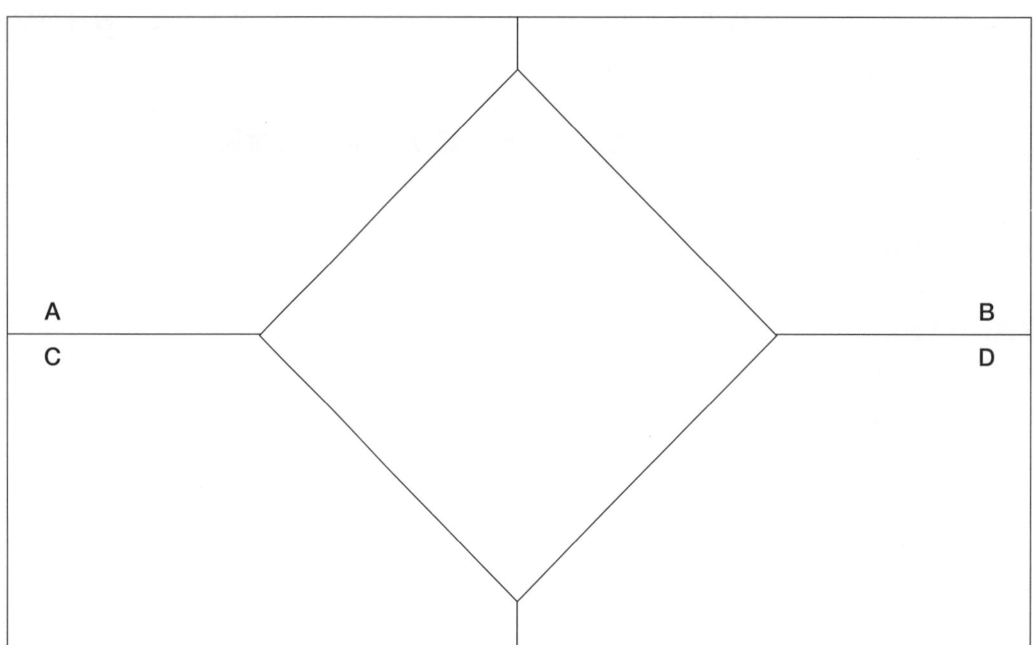

Activity 12 すらすら読もう Read Fluently

Read the article (Activity 3) to your partner. Pay attention to pronunciation, intonation, and tempo as you read aloud.

Activity 13 要約しよう Let's Summarize!

Summarize the article(s) in Japanese.

4 日本語でやってみよう Let's Show What We Can Do!

私の家族の話 My Family Story (Draft Writing)

You have learned about one immigrant family's experieneces. Your task is to draft your family story in a published story collection for Japanese students to learn about immigration to the U.S. Use the "My Family's Immigration Stories" (Activity 3-1) as a model.

Required

- □ ～たくても、～
- □【Purpose】に来ました／行きました。
- □ ～ていました／ています。

Optional

- □ ～させられました。（Causative-Passive Form）
- □ なぜなら／その理由は、～からです。
- □ まず、～
- □ 次に、～

Introduction/Hook

Family Members

Key Events in Family History (struggles, meetings, etc.)

Current Lifestyle

Conclusion (future plan, dream)

Unit 4
Final Task

日本語でアクション！
Take Action in Japanese!

私の家族の話 My Family Story

Task Sheet & Rubrics 

Personal stories have the power to move people. Your task is to share your family story in a published story collection "*Our Immigration Stories*" for Japanese students to learn about your unique immigration stories.

Your Role & Purpose	Contributing author for book publication
Your Audience	Japanese high school students
Language	☐ Describe family members ☐ Describe key events in your family history that led to where your family is today ☐ Details about each event, including dates, locations, feelings, hardships, etc. ☐ Reflection/comparison of your family in the past and currently
Product	**Product Type:** ☐ Story page (minimum 1 page) with photos ☐ PDF file posted to online **Optional:** ☐ Story Jumper

Unit 5 ともに生きる社会 Diverse Society

How do our personal and national identities influence our lives?

Lesson 1 変わりゆく日本 Evolving Japan

Essential Questions:

- How is Japan adapting to diverse cultures?
- Can diversity benefit a society?

Can-do List:

- ☐ Investigate reasons foreigners move to Japan
- ☐ Address the recent changes in Japan in regards to race, nationality, language etc.
- ☐ Describe benefits and challenges of diversity

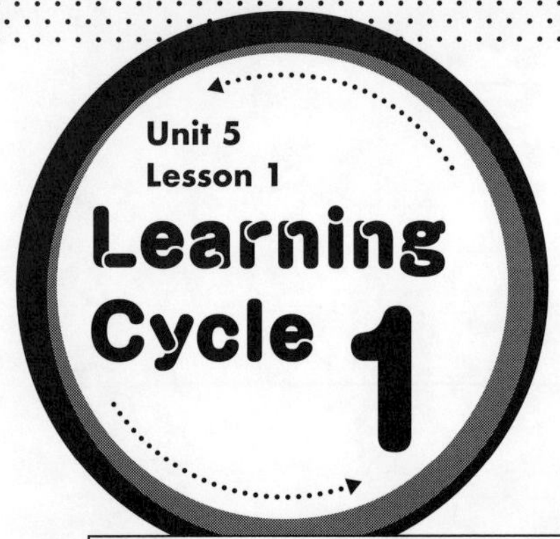

日本に住む理由

Reasons for Living in Japan

How is Japan adapting to diverse cultures? In this learning cycle, first you will learn about Multicultural Japan. Then, you will discuss with your classmates the reasons why people are coming and living in Japan. Finally you will write a short article about those reasons and give your opinion.

0 考えてみよう Let's Explore!

What do you notice in the title picture? (p.173) What ideas come to your mind when you think about the topic? Jot down keywords in Japanese below.

日本に住みたい理由

1 探ってみよう Investigate the World

Activity 1 文化の窓 Take a Look into Japanese Culture

PPT

Listen to Sensei's presentation twice. First, take notes on general ideas in English. When you listen a second time, jot down keywords in Japanese.

日本に住む理由（にほん す りゆう） Reasons for Living in Japan

What is this information about?	
Keywords in Japanese	

まとめてみよう Graphic Organizer

Demonstrate your understanding of the previous presentation by organizing your ideas below.

2 いろいろな視点を学ぼう Recognize Diverse Perspectives

読んで学ぼう（よ まな） Read and Learn

1 読んでみよう（よ） Let's Read!

Read and annotate the article below. Then, answer the following comprehension questions.

日本に住む理由 Reasons for Living in Japan

日本に住む外国人の数は年々増えている。出入国在留管理庁*の調査によると、2021年6月現在、約290万人、194の国の人々が日本に住んでいるそうだ。日本の人口の約2％が外国人ということになる。この調査によると、日本に住む外国人の一番多い国籍は、1位が中国、2位がベトナム、3位が韓国だった。この10年で特に増えているのが、ベトナムやネパールだそうだ。

多くの外国人が日本に住む理由は何だろうか。ある新聞のアンケートによると、「技術や日本語を学びたいから」「日本の文化にあこがれていたから」「お金を稼ぎやすいから」「住みやすく治安がいいから」「家族や日本に行った人にすすめられたから」「日本人はまじめで優しいから」「ほかの国より行きやすかったから」などの理由だそうだ。

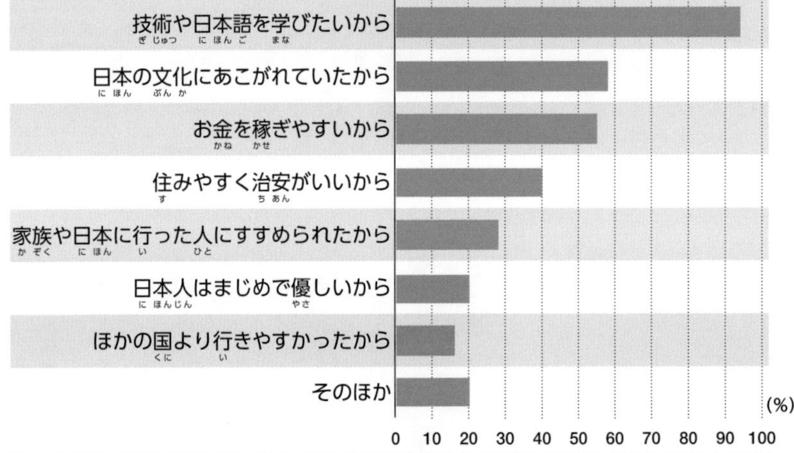

日本に住むほとんどの外国人は、「働く」か「学ぶ」ために日本に来ている。そして、その数は今後も増えていくだろう。そんな中、日本の受け入れ態勢は整っているだろうか。多文化共生社会の実現のために、日本人一人ひとりが考えるときにきている。

* **出入国在留管理庁** Immigration Services Agency

1) What is the percentage of foreigners living in Japan as of 2021?

2) What are the top three groups of foreign nationals in Japan?

3) What are some of the main reasons why people moved to Japan?

4) What does the article suggest the readers to do?

ことばリスト

□理由 □外国人 □年々 □調査 □～現在 □ある～ □技術 □学ぶ □文化 □あこがれる
□(お金を)稼ぐ □治安(がいい) □(日本を)すすめる □まじめ □受け入れ態勢 □(態勢が)整う
□多文化共生社会 □実現

2 ランキング Ranking

Write the keywords in the order of your preference or importance.

アンケートのランキング	私のランキング
1位：技術や日本語を学びたいから	1位：
2位：日本の文化にあこがれていたから	2位：
3位：お金を稼ぎやすいから	3位：
4位：住みやすく治安がいいから	4位：
5位：家族や日本に行った人にすすめられたから	5位：
6位：日本人はまじめで優しいから	6位：
7位：ほかの国より行きやすかったから	7位：

Activity 4 ペアでシェアしよう Pair Share

Share your understanding from the previous activities with your partner.

例）このアンケートによると、日本に住む理由の１位は「技術や日本語を学びたいから」ですが、私の１位は、「住みやすく治安がいいから」です。

Activity 5 グループでシェアしよう Group Share

Converse with your group members about the topic in Japanese.

例）このアンケートによると、日本に住む理由の１位は「技術や日本語を学びたいから」ですが、私の１位は、「住みやすく治安がいいから」です。

質問に答えよう　Respond to the Questions

Answer the following questions based on what you have read about the topic.

例）調査によると、2021年6月現在、日本に住む外国人の数はどのぐらいですか。
約290万人、194の国の人々が日本に住んでいるそうです。

1）調査によると、日本に住む一番多い外国人の国籍は何ですか。

2）アンケートによると、日本に来る理由の1位は何ですか。

3）記事によると、日本に住むほとんどの外国人は、何のために日本に来ましたか。

3 アイデアを交換しよう　Communicate Ideas

文法パターンを見つけよう　Let's Explore Language Structure!

1 聞いてみよう　Let's Listen!

PPT

Listen to Sensei's presentation and jot down key ideas.

2 新しい文法パターンは？　Where is a New Language Structure?

What is the common language structure? Highlight below.

- 出入国在留管理庁の調査によると、2021年6月現在、約290万人、194の国の人々が日本に住んでいるそうだ。
- この調査によると、日本に住む外国人の一番多い国籍は、1位が中国、2位がベトナム、3位が韓国だった。
- アンケートによると、「技術や日本語を学びたいから」が日本に住む理由だそうだ。

3 意味は？ What Could It Mean?

Discuss possible meanings of the language structure as a class.

4 使い方は？ How Can We Use It?

Discuss possible ways to use the language structure as a class.

5 使ってみよう Let's Use the New Language Structure!

Use the language structure in new situations.

例）記事：日本に住む理由は「技術や日本語を学びたいから」です。

➡ 記事によると、日本に住む理由は「技術や日本語を学びたいから」だそうだ。

1） 先生：日本語のクラスの学生は漢字が好きです。

➡ ....

2） ネットの記事：若者の中でスマホ依存症が増えています。

➡ ....

3） ＿＿＿＿＿＿ ： ＿＿＿＿＿＿＿＿＿＿＿＿＿＿＿＿＿＿

➡ ....

Activity 8 書いてみよう Write It Out

Express your ideas in writing using the new language structure.

私の調査：外国人が日本に行く理由

-
-
-

Activity 9

ペアでシェアしよう Pair Share

Share your ideas with your partner using the writings from the previous activity.

例) A: ○○さんの調査によると、多くの人が日本に行く理由は何ですか。

B: ネットの記事によると、理由は「技術や日本語を学びたいから」だそうです。

＿＿＿＿＿さんの調査：外国人が日本に行く理由

-
-
-

Activity 10

まとめてみよう Organize Discussion

Organize your discussion with your partner in Japanese.

Activity 11
ディスカッションしよう　Group Discussion

Discuss the topic in groups in Japanese. Use the graphic organizer to capture members' ideas, opinions, and feelings. As you listen to members' ideas, jot down key information in the graphic organizer. Finally, write down the commonalities in the middle section.

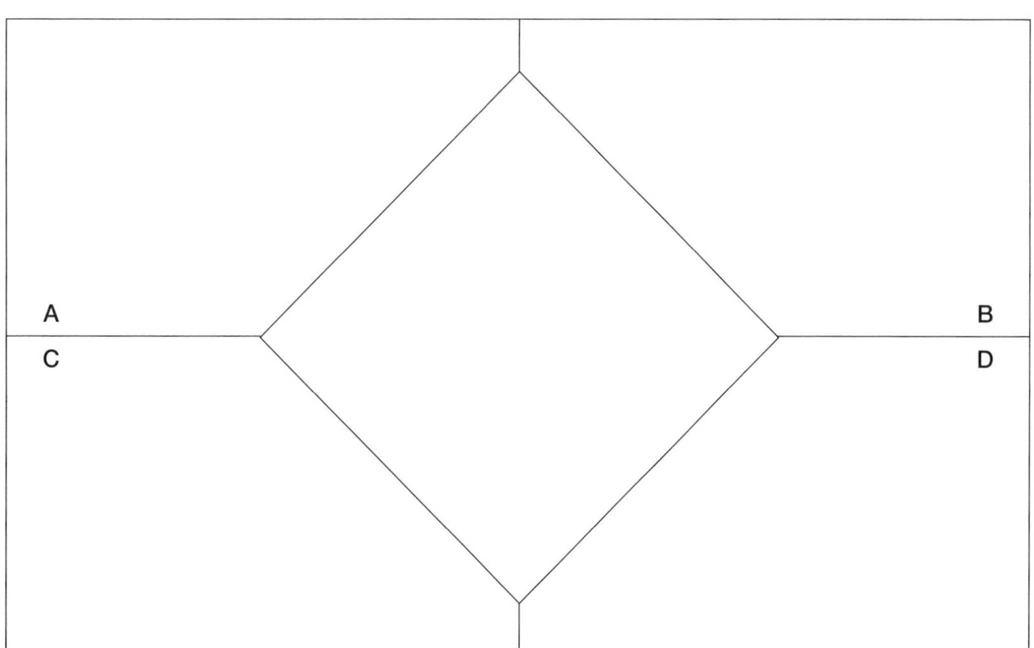

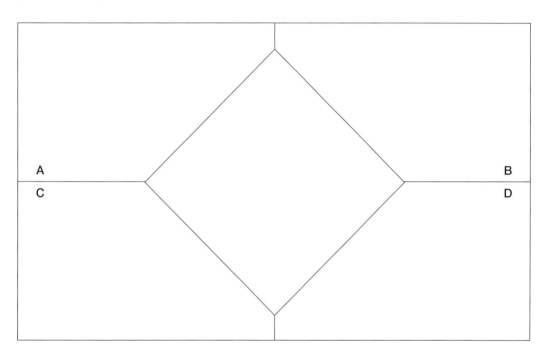

Activity 12
すらすら読もう　Read Fluently

Read the article (Activity 3) to your partner. Pay attention to pronunciation, intonation, and tempo as you read aloud.

Activity 13
要約しよう　Let's Summarize!

Summarize the article(s) in Japanese.

4 日本語でやってみよう Let's Show What We Can Do!

外国人が日本に住む理由

Reasons Foreigners Living in Japan (Article)

What are the reasons for foreigners to live in Japan? In order for Japanese high school students to become aware of the current diversity communinty situation in Japan, write a short article on the data you researched about foreigners living in Japan. Lastly, give your opinion on the reasons living in foreign countries, and why you think so. Your report should be in a formal written language, and you may use phrases from below to help draft your summary.

Required

- ☐ ～によると、～そうです。

Optional

- ☐ 私の意見では、～
- ☐ ～と思います。
- ☐ まず／最初に、～
- ☐ 次に、～

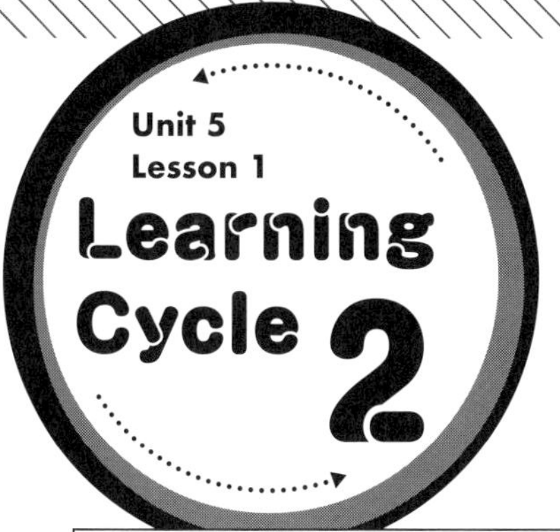

多文化共生社会：日本

Multi-Cultural Society Japan

Can diversity benefit a society? Japan tends to be seen as monocultural. However, in recent years it has begun to experience a change. In this learning cycle, first you will brainstorm the meaning of "diversity" and its impact on society. Then, you will discuss with your classmates the benefits and challenges of becoming a diverse society. Finally, you will write a news report about possible ways to embrace challenges in the midst of social changes.

0 考えてみよう Let's Explore!

1 What ideas come to your mind when you think about the topic? Jot down keywords in Japanese below.

多文化共生社会

2 What are some benefits and challenges of living in a diverse society?

1 探ってみよう Investigate the World

Activity 1 文化の窓 Take a Look into Japanese Culture

Listen to Sensei's presentation twice. First, take notes on general ideas in English. When you listen a second time, jot down keywords in Japanese.

多文化共生社会：日本 Multi-Cultural Society Japan

What is this information about?	
Keywords in Japanese	

Activity 2 まとめてみよう Graphic Organizer

Demonstrate your understanding of the previous presentation by organizing your ideas below.

2 いろいろな視点を学ぼう Recognize Diverse Perspectives

Activity 3 読んで学ぼう Read and Learn

1 読んでみよう Let's Read!

Read and annotate the article below. Then, answer the following comprehension questions.

多文化共生社会：日本 Multi-Cultural Society Japan

「ダイバーシティ」とは、「多様性を表し、性別、国籍、人種、年齢などさまざまな違いを問わず、多様な人材を認め、活用すること」である。日本でも、女性や高齢者、外国人や障害のある人など、多様性を認めて、その人の特性を活かすようになってきている。

多様性のメリットは、広く優秀な人材が見つけられることだ。違う文化や意見に触れ、価値観や視野が広がることで、今までにないものを生み出す可能性がある。また、一人ひとりが認められることで、自信ややりがいも生まれる。

一方で、多様性が広がると、考え方や価値観の違いから、コミュニケーション・ギャップが起こる。その結果、衝突することもある。また、一部の人が優遇されているという不満が生まれる可能性もある。

日本では今、多くの外国人労働者や留学生が生活し、長期滞在者や観光客も増えている。多様性のある社会を目指して、私たちは、違いを受け入れ、お互いを尊重し、ともに生きていく努力をしていく必要がある。

1) What are some keywords from the definition of diversity?

2) What are the merits of diversity?

3) What are the possible challenges of a diverse society?

4) What does the article suggest the readers do in order to have a successful diverse society?

ことばリスト

□多様性 □(多様性を)表す □性別 □(違いを)問わず □多様な □人材 □活用する

□障害(のある) □特性 □(特性を)活かす □広い □優秀な □(意見に)触れる □視野(が広がる)

□生み出す □可能性 □自信 □やりがい □衝突する □一部 □優遇する □不満 □労働者

□留学生 □長期滞在者 □目指す □(違いを)受け入れる □尊重する □ともに □努力(をする)

2 チェックリスト Checklist

Check off the keywords that apply to the information presented above.

	メリット	デメリット
例) 価値観や視野が広がる。	✓	
1) 衝突が起こる。		
2) 一人ひとりが認められ、自信ややりがいが生まれる。		
3) 広く優秀な人材が見つけられる。		
4) コミュニケーション・ギャップが起こる。		
5) 今までにないものを生み出せる。		
6) 一部の人が優遇されているという不満が生まれる。		

Activity 4
ペアでシェアしよう Pair Share

Share your understanding from the previous activities with your partner.

例) 多様性のメリットは、広く優秀な人材が見つけられることだと思います。

Activity 5
グループでシェアしよう Group Share

Converse with your group members about the topic in Japanese.

例) 多様性のメリットは、広く優秀な人材が見つけられることだと思います。

Activity 6
質問に答えよう　Respond to the Questions

Answer the following questions based on what you have read about the topic.

例）多様性のメリットは、何ですか。

広く優秀な人材が見つけられることだと思います。

1）多様性のメリットは、何ですか。

2）多様性のデメリットは、何ですか。

3 アイデアを交換しよう　Communicate Ideas

Activity 7
文法パターンを見つけよう　Let's Explore Language Structure!

1 聞いてみよう　Let's Listen!

PPT

Listen to Sensei's presentation and jot down key ideas.

2 新しい文法パターンは？　Where is a New Language Structure?

What is the common language structure? Highlight below.

- 障害のある人
- 今までにないものを生み出す可能性
- 一部の人が優遇されているという不満
- 多様性のある社会

3 意味は？　What Could It Mean?

Discuss possible meanings of the language structure as a class.

4 使い方は？ How Can We Use It?

Discuss possible ways to use the language structure as a class.

5 使ってみよう Let's Use the New Language Structure!

Use the language structure in new situations.

名詞 (Noun)	くわしく説明する (Descriptive)	もっとくわしく説明する (More Descriptive)
例) 人材	優秀な人材	若くて優秀な人材
1) 人		
2) 社会		
3) もの		
4) こと		
5) 場所		

Activity 8 書いてみよう Write It Out

Express your ideas in writing using the new language structure.

私の意見：多様性のある社会について

メリット	デメリット
• • •	• • •

Activity 9

ペアでシェアしよう Pair Share

Share your ideas with your partner using the writings from the previous activity.

例) A: 多様性のある社会には、どんなメリットとデメリットがあると思いますか。

B: 私の意見では、広く優秀な人材が見つけられるというメリットがあると思います。一方で、衝突が起こるというデメリットがあると思います。

＿＿＿＿＿さんの意見：多様性のある社会について

メリット	デメリット
• • •	• • •

Activity 10

まとめてみよう Organize Discussion

Organize your discussion with your partner in Japanese.

Activity 11
ディスカッションしよう Group Discussion

Discuss the topic in groups in Japanese. Use the graphic organizer to capture members' ideas, opinions, and feelings. As you listen to members' ideas, jot down key information in the graphic organizer. Finally, write down the commonalities in the middle section.

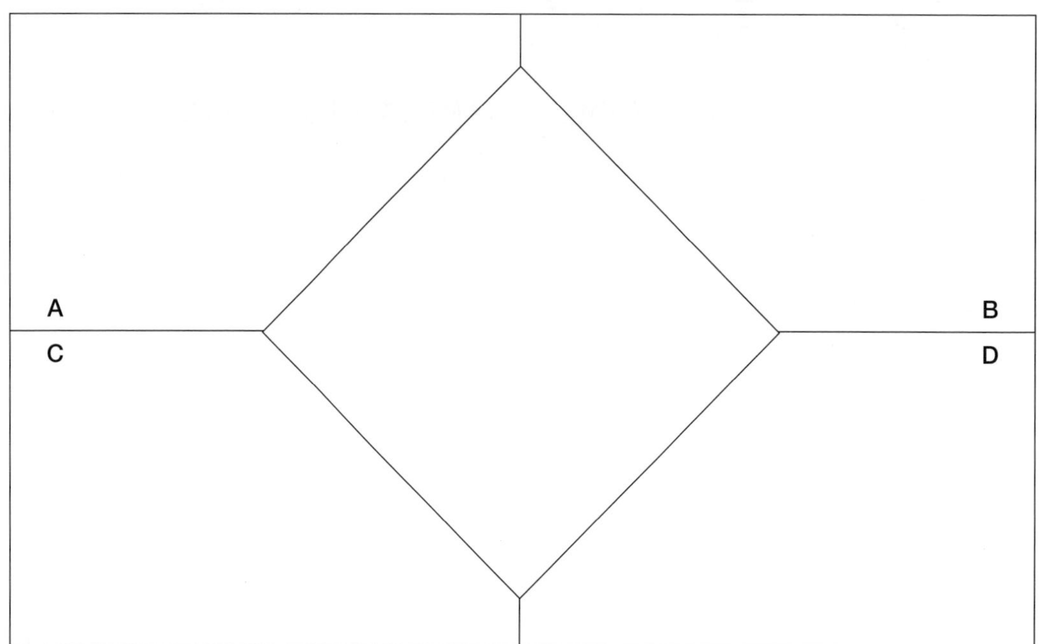

Activity 12
すらすら読もう Read Fluently

Read the article (Activity 3) to your partner. Pay attention to pronunciation, intonation, and tempo as you read aloud.

Activity 13
要約しよう Let's Summarize!

Summarize the article(s) in Japanese.

4 日本語でやってみよう Let's Show What We Can Do!

多様性のある社会のメリットとデメリット

Merits and Demerits of Diverstiy Society (Opinion)

What are the benefits and the challenges of having diversity? Write a short column for a local Japanese newspaper on the benefits of diversity as well as challenges that may occur with it. Lastly, give your opinion on the importance of diversity, and why you think so. Your report should be in a formal written language, and you may use phrases from below to help draft your summary.

Required

- □ Modified Nouns
- □ ～によると、～そうです。
- □ 一方で、～

Optional

- □ 私の意見では、～
- □ ～と思います。
- □ なぜなら／その理由は、～からです。
- □ まず／最初に、～
- □ 次に、～

Unit 4
Mid Task

日本語でアクション！
Take Action in Japanese!

多文化共生社会：日本

Local Government on Diverse Society Japan (Opinion)

You have learned about the reasons foreigners living in Japan and benefits and challenges of diverse community. You will write a letter to a Japanese local government to raise awareness on the increasing diversity in Japan. Start by addressing the recent changes in Japan in regards to diversity. You should include information that you have gained in this lesson, as well as additional information to support your opinion. Lastly, conclude your presentation with possible ways to embrace challenges in the midst of social changes.

Unit 5 ともに生きる社会 Diverse Society

How do our personal and national identities influence our lives?

Lesson 2 アイデンティティ Identity

Essential Questions:

- What are diverse community members' experiences in Japan?
- What is our cultural identity?

Can-do List:

- ☐ Identify mixed-race people's challenges in Japan
- ☐ Describe the issues and struggles for mixed-race people in Japan
- ☐ Discuss equality for all identities
- ☐ Introduce their own "identity" story

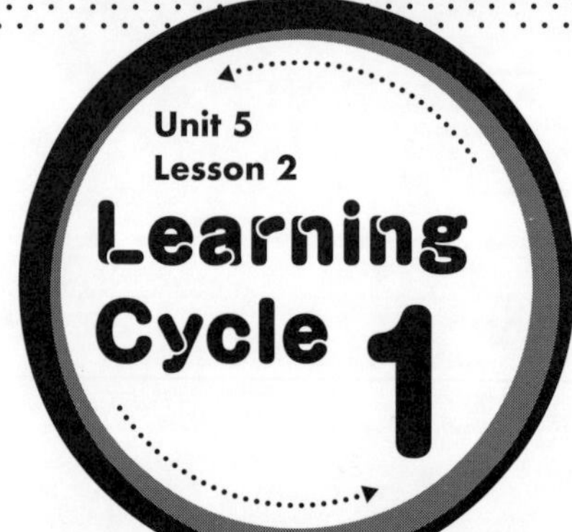

ハーフ？ ミックス？ ダブル？

The Mixed-Race Experience in Japan

What are diverse community members' experiences in Japan? In this learning cycle, first you will learn about the experiences of diverse community members living in Japan. Then, you will discuss the difficulties they face and brainstorm ways to create a better living environment for all people in Japan. Lastly, you will write a short essay to raise awareness about the experiences of diverse community members in Japan, and give possible ways to create an inclusive community for all.

0 考えてみよう Let's Explore!

What do you notice in the title picture? (p.193) What ideas come to your mind when you think about the topic? Jot down keywords in Japanese below.

外国人（がいこくじん）

1 探ってみよう Investigate the World

Activity 1

文化の窓（ぶんかのまど） Take a Look into Japanese Culture

PPT

Listen to Sensei's presentation twice. First, take notes on general ideas in English. When you listen a second time, jot down keywords in Japanese.

ハーフ？ ミックス？ ダブル？ The Mixed-Race Experience in Japan

What is this information about?	
Keywords in Japanese	

Activity 2

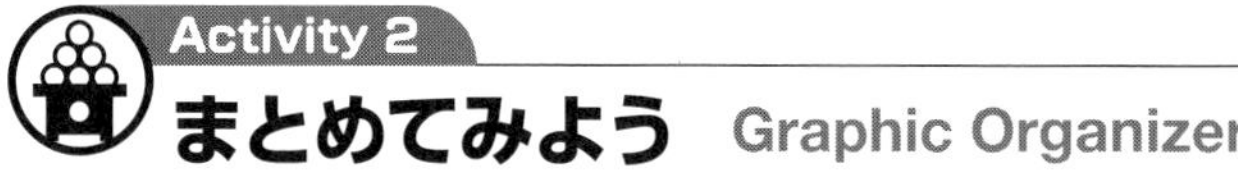

まとめてみよう Graphic Organizer

Demonstrate your understanding of the previous presentation by organizing your ideas below.

2 いろいろな視点を学ぼう Recognize Diverse Perspectives

Activity 3 読んで学ぼう Read and Learn

1 読んでみよう Let's Read!

Read and annotate the article below. Then, answer the following comprehension questions.

ハーフ？ ミックス？ ダブル？

The Mixed-Race Experience in Japan

日本では、一般的に両親の一人が外国人のとき、その子どもを「ハーフ」と呼びます。でも、「ハーフ」は、半分という意味でマイナスのイメージが強いので、「ハーフ」という言葉は使うべきではないという意見があります。代わりに、倍という意味の「ダブル」や、混ざっているという意味の「ミックス」を使うべきだという人もいます。

言葉の持つ意味や影響を考え、使う言葉を見直すことは大切です。しかし、ただ言い換えればいいというものではありません。彼らは、見た目が違うことや両親の一人が日本人ではないというだけで、「国籍はどこですか？」「日本語が上手ですね」「外国語で話して」などと言われることもあるそうです。言った人たちには悪気はなく、なんとなく言ってしまったということもあるでしょう。しかし、彼らの中には「なんでそんなことを言われるのだろう」と重く受けとめ、居場所が見つけられず、つらくなってしまうこともあるそうです。

私たちは、このような状況をどう受けとめるべきでしょうか。その人がどんな考え方やルーツを持っているのか、お互いが理解し、尊重することで、呼び方に対する受けとめ方も変わっていくのではないでしょうか。

1) How are racially mixed people addressed in Japan?

2) What is the author's opinion about the use of "Half"?

3) According to the author, what types of comments make the mixed-raced Japanese individuals feel like outsiders?

4) What does the author suggest the readers do in order to address mixed-raced Japanese people?

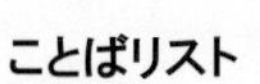

□一般的 □半分 □倍 □混ざる □見直す □言い換える □悪気(はない) □なんとなく

□受けとめる □居場所 □状況 □ルーツ □理解する □尊重する □呼び方 □受けとめ方

2 正しい？間違い？ True and False

Read the statements. Write true (○) or false (×) accordingly.

例)「ハーフ」という言葉を使うべきだという意見がある。	×
1)「ミックス」や「ダブル」という言葉を使うべきだという意見がある。	
2)「ハーフ」を「ミックス」や「ダブル」という言葉に言い換えるべきだ。	
3) 言葉の持つ意味や影響を考えるべきだ。	
4) 使う言葉を見直すべきではない。	
5) その人がどんな考え方やルーツを持っているのか考えるべきだ。	

Activity 4 ペアでシェアしよう Pair Share

Share your understanding from the previous activities with your partner.

例) この記事によると、「ミックス」や「ダブル」という言葉を使うべきだという意見があります。

Activity 5 グループでシェアしよう Group Share

Converse with your group members about the topic in Japanese.

例) この記事によると、「ミックス」や「ダブル」という言葉を使うべきだという意見があります。

Activity 6
質問に答えよう Respond to the Questions

Answer the following questions based on what you have read about the topic.

例) 多文化共生社会のために、どんなことをするべきだと思いますか。
その人がどんな考え方やルーツを持っているのか考えるべきだと思います。

1) 多文化共生社会のために、どんなことをするべきだと思いますか。

2) 多文化共生社会のために、どんなことをするべきではないと思いますか。

3 アイデアを交換しよう Communicate Ideas

Activity 7
文法パターンを見つけよう Let's Explore Language Structure!

1 聞いてみよう Let's Listen!

PPT

Listen to Sensei's presentation and jot down key ideas.

2 新しい文法パターンは？ Where is a New Language Structure?

What is the common language structure? Highlight below.

- 「ハーフ」という言葉は使うべきではないという意見があります。
- 混ざっているという意味の「ミックス」を使うべきだという人もいます。
- 私たちは、このような状況をどう受けとめるべきでしょうか。

3 意味は？ What Could It Mean?

Discuss possible meanings of the language structure as a class.

4 使い方は？ How Can We Use It?

Discuss possible ways to use the language structure as a class.

5 使ってみよう Let's Use the New Language Structure!

Use the language structure in new situations.

例) A: もっと日本語が上手になりたいです。
B: それなら、ちゃんと宿題をするべきだと思いますよ。

1) A: いろいろな人と友だちになりたいです。
B: ....

2) A: もっと相手のことを理解したいです。
B: ....

3) A: 平和な世界をつくりたいです。
B: ....

Activity 8 書いてみよう Write It Out

Express your ideas in writing using the new language structure.

私の意見：お互いを理解するために

するべきこと	するべきではないこと
•	•
•	•
•	•

Activity 9
ペアでシェアしよう Pair Share

Share your ideas with your partner using the writings from the previous activity.

例）A: 私たちはお互いを理解するために、何をするべきだと思いますか。

B: その人がどんな考え方やルーツを持っているのか考えるべきだと思います。

＿＿＿＿＿さんの意見：お互いを理解するために

するべきこと	するべきではないこと
• • •	• • •

Activity 10
まとめてみよう Organize Discussion

Organize your discussion with your partner in Japanese.

Activity 11 ディスカッションしよう Group Discussion

Discuss the topic in groups in Japanese. Use the graphic organizer to capture members' ideas, opinions, and feelings. As you listen to members' ideas, jot down key information in the graphic organizer. Finally, write down the commonalities in the middle section.

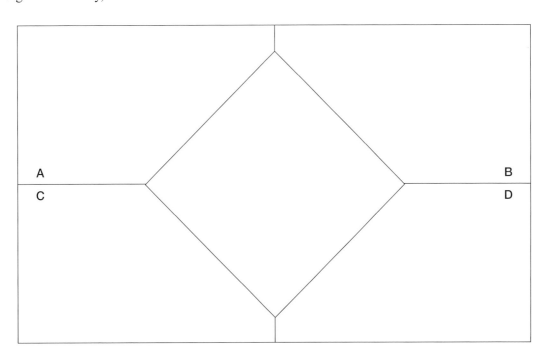

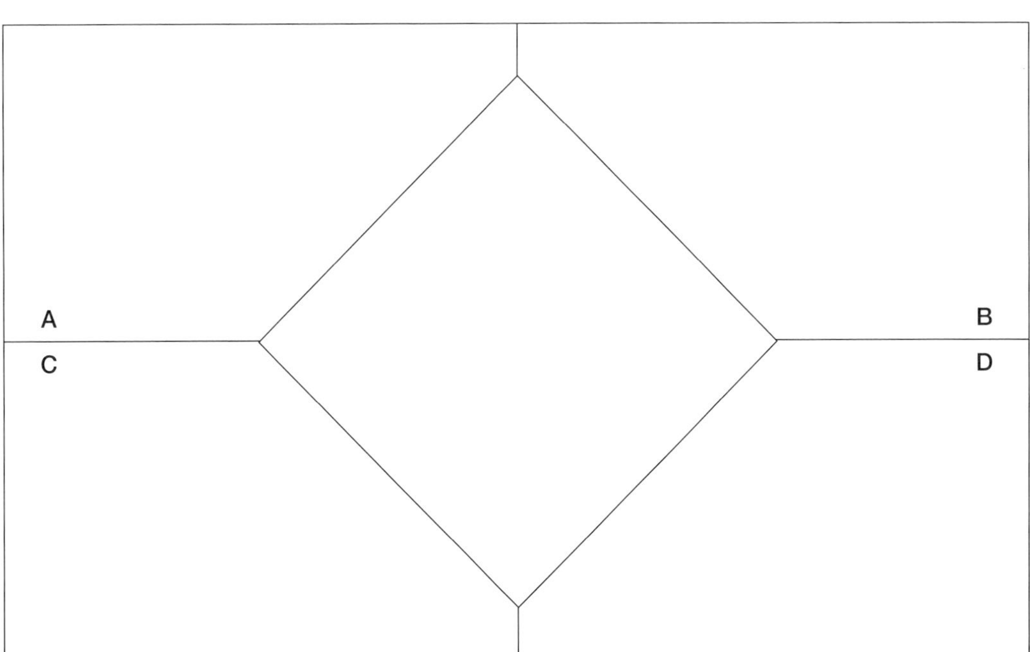

Activity 12 すらすら読もう Read Fluently

Read the article (Activity 3) to your partner. Pay attention to pronunciation, intonation, and tempo as you read aloud.

Activity 13 要約しよう Let's Summarize!

Summarize the article(s) in Japanese.

4 日本語でやってみよう Let's Show What We Can Do!

多文化共生社会について Multi-Cultural Society (Essay)

Raise awareness about the experiences of diverse community members in Japan by writing a short essay for Japanese high school students. Start by sharing what you've learned about the current situation of diverse community members in Japan. Then, state the things we must/must not do in order to create a better living environment for them. Lastly, provide an example of the experience of diverse community members in your town and give possible ways to create an inclusive community for all.

Required

- ☐ ～べきだと思います／べきではないと思います。
- ☐ 私の意見では、～

Optional

- ☐ まず／最初に、～
- ☐ 次に、～

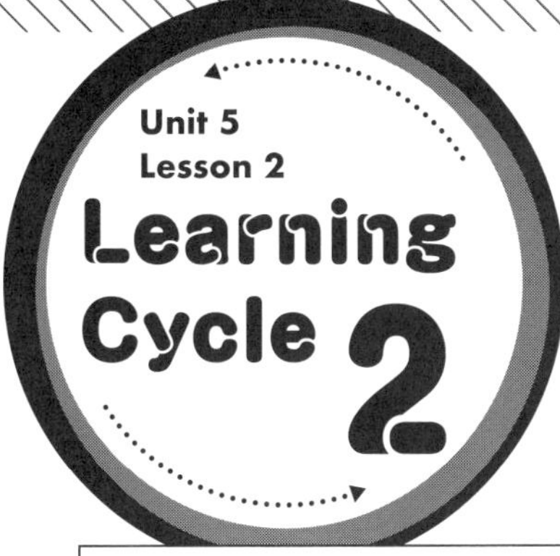

私のアイデンティティ
わたし

My Identity

What is our identity? In this learning cycle, first, you will read a personal identity story of a Filipino immigrant in Japan. Then, you will discuss his identity experiences with your classmates. Finally, you will express your identity by creating a poem and introducing it in a podcast.

0 考えてみよう Let's Explore!

What ideas come to your mind when you think about the topic? Jot down keywords in Japanese below.

アイデンティティ

1 探ってみよう Investigate the World

Activity 1 文化の窓 Take a Look into Japanese Culture
ぶんか まど

Listen to Sensei's presentation twice. First, take notes on general ideas in English. When you listen a second time, jot down keywords in Japanese.

私のアイデンティティ　My Identity

What is this information about?	
Keywords in Japanese	

Activity 2 まとめてみよう　Graphic Organizer

Demonstrate your understanding of the previous presentation by organizing your ideas below.

2 いろいろな視点を学ぼう　Recognize Diverse Perspectives

Activity 3 読んで学ぼう　Read and Learn

1 読んでみよう　Let's Read!

Read and annotate the article below. Then, answer the following comprehension questions.

私のアイデンティティ　My Identity

ジェリコさんのお母さんはフィリピン出身で、1980年代に日本に働きに来ました。そして、日本人の男性と結婚して、ジェリコさんが生まれました。ジェリコさんは、小学校に入るまで、お母さんとはタガログ語で話していました。ジェリコさんのお母さんはとても明るい人で、ジェリコさんはお母さんのことが大好きでした。

1) Why did Jericho's mother move to Japan?

でも、小学校に入って、お母さんとあまり話さなくなりました。友だちに「お母さん、ちょっと変わってるね」と言われたことがショックだったからです。みんなと違うのが嫌で、お母さんのこともフィリピンのことも、タガログ語も嫌いになりました。

ジェリコさんには、名前が二つあります。フィリピンの名前「ジェリコ」と日本の名前「たける」です。中学生になったとき、ジェリコさんはクラスの自己紹介で「たける」と言って、その後も日本の名前を使うようになりました。自分が日本人とフィリピン人のハーフだということを知られたくなかったからです。

高校生になって、ジェリコさんはタガログ語がほとんど話せなくなっていました。ジェリコさんは人と話すのが苦手で、家にも学校にも自分の居場所がないように感じていました。そんなジェリコさんを救ったのが、詩を書くことでした。ハーフで障害のある人が詩を書いているという記事を読んで、ジェリコさんも詩を書き始めたのです。詩を書くということは、自分と向き合うことでした。ジェリコさんは、お母さんの国フィリピンのことをもっと知りたくなりました。

大学生になったジェリコさんは、タガログ語を学ぶためにフィリピンに留学しました。半分はフィリピン人なのにタガログ語ができないのは恥ずかしいと思ったからです。ジェリコさんの今の夢は、将来、日本とフィリピンで詩人になることです。

『自分の虹』by ジェリコ

自分ってなんだろうか
山のように変わらないものだろうか
川のように流れるものだろうか

自分ってなんだろうか
見つけるものなのだろうか
人が決めるものなのだろうか
作り上げるものなのだろうか

いつか自分の虹を探そう

2) Why did Jericho stop speaking his home language at school?

3) What struggles did Jericho go through when he was young?

4) What gave him motivation when he was in high school?

5) What inspired Jericho to be creative?

6) List words from the lyrics that describe Jericho's identity.

ことばリスト

☐明るい（人） ☐変わっている ☐ショック ☐嫌 ☐自己紹介 ☐知られる ☐救う ☐詩
☐書き始める ☐向き合う ☐留学する ☐恥ずかしい ☐将来 ☐詩人 ☐虹 ☐流れる ☐作り上げる
☐いつか

2 順番に並べよう Sequencing

Write the keywords in the appropriate order of events or steps.

（　　A　　）⇒（　　　　　　）⇒（　　　　　　）

⇒（　　　　　　）⇒（　　　　　　）⇒（　　　　　　）

A. お母さんとタガログ語で話していた。
B. 詩を書き始めた。
C. 日本の名前を使うようになった。
D. タガログ語を学ぶためにフィリピンに留学した。
E. お母さんとあまり話さなくなった。
F. タガログ語がほとんど話せなくなっていた。

Activity 4 ペアでシェアしよう Pair Share

Share your understanding from the previous activities with your partner.

例）ジェリコさんは、小学校に入るまで、お母さんとタガログ語で話していました。

Activity 5 グループでシェアしよう Group Share

Converse with your group members about the topic in Japanese.

例）ジェリコさんは、小学校に入るまで、お母さんとタガログ語で話していました。

Activity 6 質問に答えよう Respond to the Questions

Answer the following questions based on what you have read about the topic.

Q: ジェリコさんは、アイデンティティをどんな言葉で表現していますか。

3 アイデアを交換しよう Communicate Ideas

Activity 7 文法パターンを見つけよう Let's Explore Language Structure!

1 聞いてみよう Let's Listen!

PPT

Listen to Sensei's presentation and jot down key ideas.

2 新しい文法パターンは？ Where is a New Language Structure?

What is the common language structure? Highlight below.

- 自分ってなんだろうか。
- 山のように変わらないものだろうか。
- 川のように流れるものだろうか。

3 意味は？ What Could It Mean?

Discuss possible meanings of the language structure as a class.

4 使い方は？ How Can We Use It?

Discuss possible ways to use the language structure as a class.

5 使ってみよう Let's Use the New Language Structure!

Use the language structure in new situations.

例) 日本語の勉強をしたら、日本の大学に行ける？

➡ 日本語の勉強をしたら、日本の大学に行けるだろうか。

1) 料理ができたら、もてる？

➡ ....

2) お金持ちだったら、幸せになれる？

➡ ....

3) たくさん言葉が話せたら、いい仕事につける？

➡ ....

Activity 8 書いてみよう Write It Out

Express your ideas in writing using the new language structure.

私がジェリコさんだったら…

・お母さんとあまり話さなくなっただろうか。	はい・いいえ
・	はい・いいえ
・	はい・いいえ
・	はい・いいえ
・	はい・いいえ

Activity 9

ペアでシェアしよう Pair Share

Share your ideas with your partner using the writings from the previous activity.

例）A: 私がジェリコさんだったら、お母さんとあまり話さなくなっただろうか…。
○○さんだったら、どうですか。

B: 私がジェリコさんだったら、お母さんと話すと思います。

__________ さんがジェリコさんだったら…

・お母さんとあまり話さなくなっただろうか。	はい・いいえ
・	はい・いいえ
・	はい・いいえ
・	はい・いいえ
・	はい・いいえ

Activity 10

まとめてみよう Organize Discussion

Organize your discussion with your partner in Japanese.

Activity 11 ディスカッションしよう Group Discussion

Discuss the topic in groups in Japanese. Use the graphic organizer to capture members' ideas, opinions, and feelings. As you listen to members' ideas, jot down key information in the graphic organizer. Finally, write down the commonalities in the middle section.

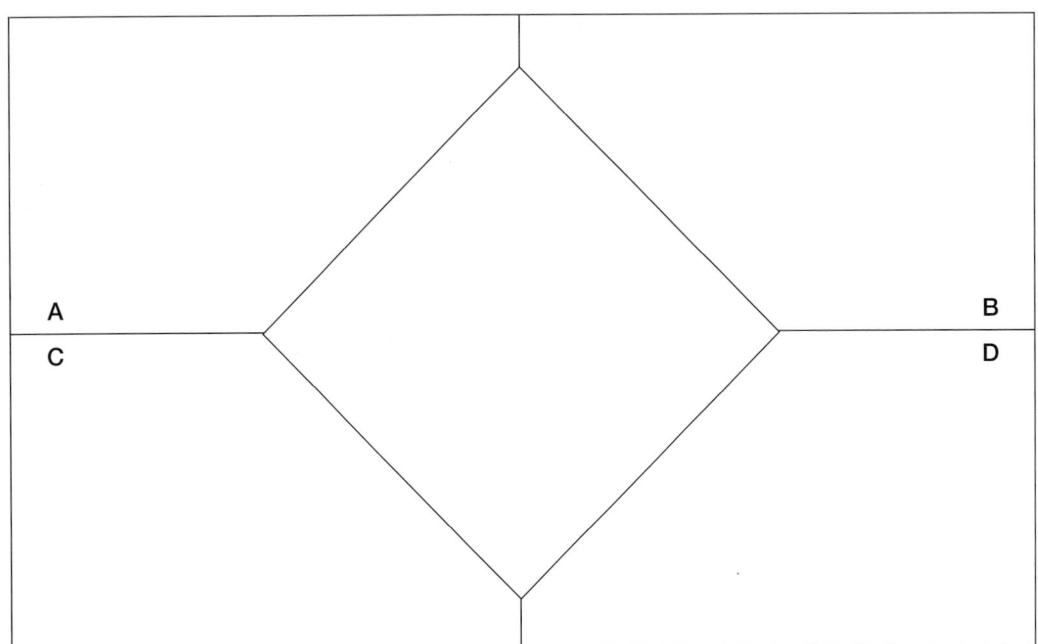

Activity 12 すらすら読もう Read Fluently

Read the article (Activity 3) to your partner. Pay attention to pronunciation, intonation, and tempo as you read aloud.

Activity 13 要約しよう Let's Summarize!

Summarize the article(s) in Japanese.

4 日本語でやってみよう Let's Show What We Can Do!

Unit 5 Lesson 2 Cycle 2

私のアイデンティティ My Identity (Poem)

Now that you have had an opportunity to learn about Jericho's identity journey, take time to consider what makes who you are in order to share your poem with "Human Rights Week" event in Japan.

1 My Identity Circle

In the middle circle, write your name. In the outside circles, list 6 words that represent your identity. These can be visible or invisible elements of your identity.

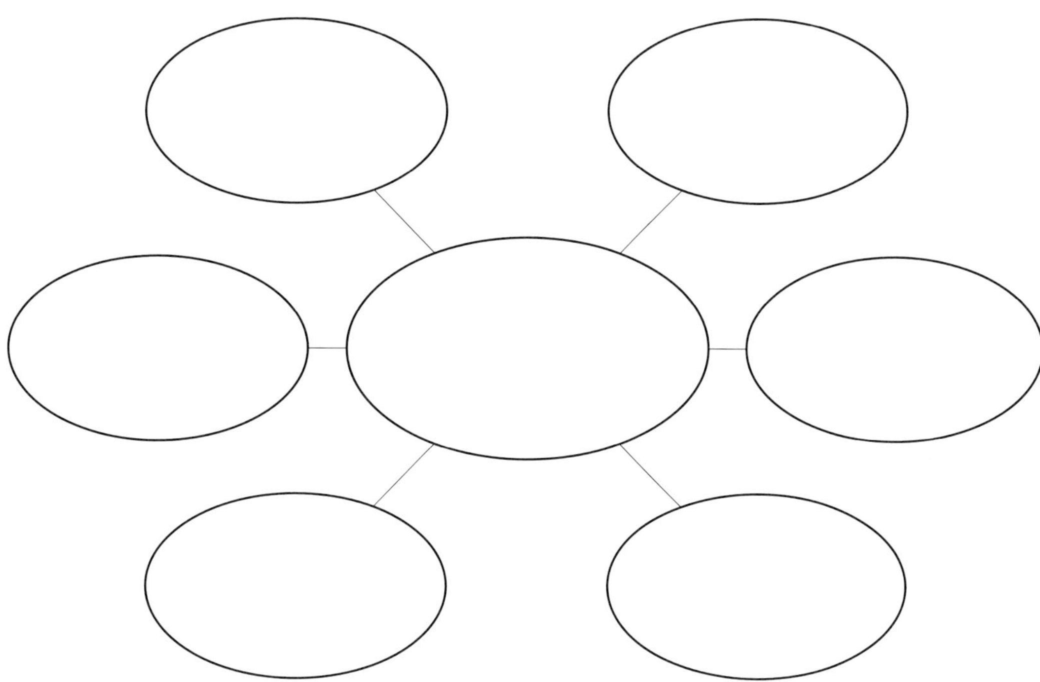

2 Poetry Writing

Write a poetry of your version of『自分の虹』using the following template:

『自分の虹』by ____________________

自分ってなんだろうか

____だろうか

それとも、____だろうか

それとも、____だろうか

Unit 5
Final Task

日本語でアクション！

Take Action in Japanese!

私のアイデンティティ　Our Identity

Task Sheet & Rubrics 

What is our identity? How is identity influenced by culture and nationality? Your task is to write a podcast on the topic of "Identity." In your podcast, you will share what you learned about the struggles with identity for racially mixed people living in Japan. Then, you will share your own story to highlight any common ground between you and those people. Reflect on your own identity by including the events in your life that have shaped who you are, and how you identify yourself today. Lastly, propose what we can do to promote equality for people of diverse backgrounds.

Your Role & Purpose	Student reflect on identity and propose ideas to promote equality for people of diverse backgrounds
Your Audience	Listeners for the podcast
Language	☐ Address issues and struggles with identity for racially mixed people in Japan ☐ Narrate your identity story ☐ Discuss your opinions on equality ☐ Propose what should be done for those who experience discrimination because of their identity
Product	**Product Type:** ☐ Blog Post (using "written formal language") **Optional:** ☐ Drawings/pictures

Unit 6 未来へのコンパス Compass to My Future

What are the elements of a "good life"?

Lesson 1 生きがい *Ikigai*

Essential Questions:

- How could we live a "good life"?
- What contributes to *Ikigai* - the purpose of life?
- Have you ever immersed yourself in doing something and lost sense of time?

Can-do List:

- ☐ Identify the elements that make *Ikigai*
- ☐ Discuss and share what my own *Ikigai* is in groups
- ☐ Describe my life events and experiences
- ☐ Analyze and describe characteristics and strengths

生きがい

Ikigai

How could we live a "good life"? What contributes to Ikigai - the purpose of life? What drives you to live life fully? In this learning cycle, you will learn elements of *Ikigai* - purpose for life. Then, you and your classmates will share your experiences. Finally, you will reflect on your life experiences based on the four elements of *Ikigai*.

0 考えてみよう Let's Explore!

What do you notice in the title picture? (p.213) What ideas come to your mind when you think about the topic? Jot down keywords in Japanese below.

生きがい

1 探ってみよう Investigate the World

Take a Look into Japanese Culture

Listen to Sensei's presentation twice. First, take notes on general ideas in English. When you listen a second time, jot down keywords in Japanese.

生きがい *Ikigai*

What is this information about?	
Keywords in Japanese	

Activity 2 まとめてみよう Graphic Organizer

Demonstrate your understanding of the previous presentation by organizing your ideas below.

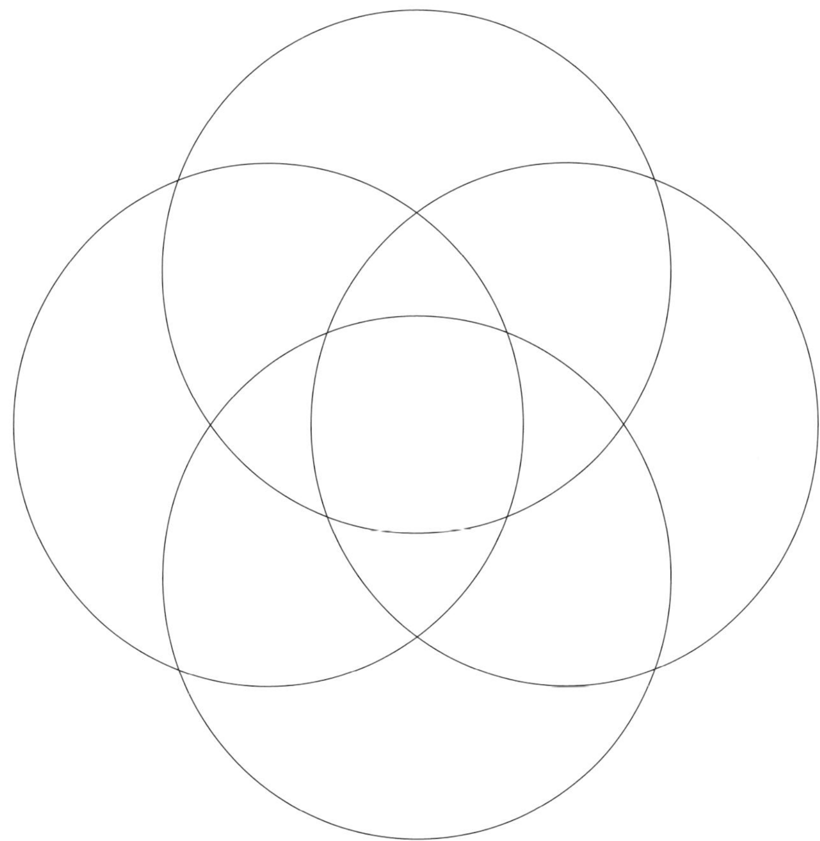

2 いろいろな視点を学ぼう Recognize Diverse Perspectives

Activity 3 読んで学ぼう Read and Learn

1 読んでみよう Let's Read!

Read and annotate the article below. Then, answer the following comprehension questions.

生きがい *Ikigai*

みなさんは、「IKIGAI（生きがい）」という言葉を聞いたことがありますか。「生きがい」とは、昔から日本にある考え方で、生きる価値や生きる喜びを感じることです。「生きがい」は、長く健康に生きるための考え方として、世界でも注目を集めるようになりました。

人はどんなときに、生きる価値や喜びを感じるのでしょうか。「好きなこと」「得意なこと」「世界が必要とすること」「お金になること」が重なったときと言われていますが、みなさんもそう思いますか。

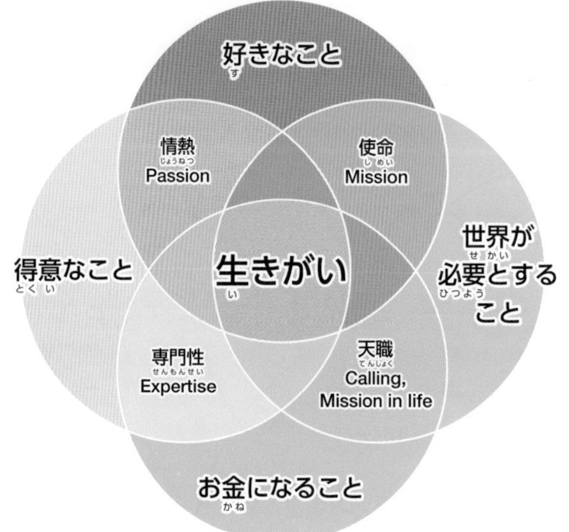

「好きなこと」とは、自分が「夢中になれること」です。みなさんは、時間を忘れて、何かに打ち込んだことがありますか。

「得意なこと」とは、「自信を持ってできること」です。スキルと才能があることと言えるでしょう。

「世界が必要とすること」とは、「人や社会のためにすること」です。ボランティア活動をして、人やコミュニティに貢献することもここに入ります。みなさんは、ボランティア活動をしたことがありますか。

「お金になること」とは、「お金を払う価値がある」ということです。自分のしたことに対して、お金を払ってもいいと思われることです。

1) What are the four elements of *Ikigai*?

-
-
-
-

2) What happens when the things you like and what you are good at intersect?

3) Your "calling" emerges when ______________ and ______________ overlap.

4) What are the words that describe the state of "flow"?

5) What is one way to find out what the world needs?

「生きがい」は人それぞれです。仕事が生きがいという人もいるでしょう。子育てが生きがいという人もいるでしょう。ペットの世話が生きがいだという人もいるでしょう。みなさんは、今、どんなことに生きがいを感じていますか。

6) What are some examples of activities people find *Ikigai* in?

ことばリスト

□喜び □(喜びを)感じる □健康 □世界 □得意な □重なる □夢中(になる) □(時間を)忘れる □打ち込む □スキル(がある) □才能(がある) □コミュニティ □貢献する □(〜に)対して □子育て

2 正しい?間違い? True and False

Read the statements. Write true (○) or false (×) accordingly.

例) 生きがいとは、昔から世界中にある考え方だ。	×
1) 人が生きがいを感じるのは、「好きなこと」「得意なこと」「世界が必要とすること」「お金になること」の4つが重なったときだ。	
2) 生きがいとは、生きる価値や喜びを感じることだ。	
3) 「好きなこと」とは、人やコミュニティに貢献することだ。	
4) 「得意なこと」とは、スキルと才能があって自信を持ってできることだ。	
5) 「世界が必要とすること」とは、自分が夢中になれることだ。	
6) 「お金になること」とは、自分のしたことに対してお金を払ってもいいと思われることだ。	
7) 「生きがい」は人それぞれ違う。	

Activity 4 ペアでシェアしよう Pair Share

Share your understanding from the previous activities with your partner.

例) 生きがいとは、生きる価値や喜びを感じることです。

Activity 5 グループでシェアしよう Group Share

Converse with your group members about the topic in Japanese.

例) 生きがいとは、生きる価値や喜びを感じることです。

Activity 6
質問に答えよう Respond to the Questions

Answer the following questions based on what you have read about the topic.

例)「お金になること」とは何ですか。

自分のしたことに対してお金を払ってもいいと思われることです。

1)「好きなこと」とは何ですか。

2)「世界が必要とすること」とは何ですか。

3)「生きがい」とは何ですか。

3 アイデアを交換しよう Communicate Ideas

Activity 7
文法パターンを見つけよう Let's Explore Language Structure!

1 聞いてみよう Let's Listen!

Listen to Sensei's presentation and jot down key ideas.

PPT

2 新しい文法パターンは? Where is a New Language Structure?

What is the common language structure? Highlight below.

- みなさんは、「IKIGAI(生きがい)」という言葉を聞いたことがありますか。
- みなさんは、時間を忘れて、何かに打ち込んだことがありますか。
- みなさんは、ボランティア活動をしたことがありますか。

3 意味は? What Could It Mean?

Discuss possible meanings of the language structure as a class.

4 使い方は？ How Can We Use It?

Discuss possible ways to use the language structure as a class.

5 使ってみよう Let's Use the New Language Structure!

Use the language structure in new situations.

例)（ 昔 ）

➡ 昔、一度だけテレビに出たことがあります。

1)（子どものとき）

➡

2)（中学生のとき）

➡

3)（高校生になってから）

➡

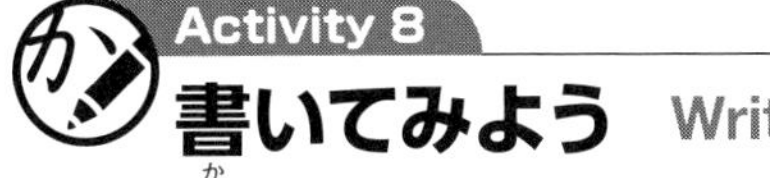

Activity 8 書いてみよう Write It Out

Express your ideas in writing using the new language structure.

私のこと

好きなこと 何かに夢中になったことがある？	
得意なこと 自信を持ってできることは何？	
世界が必要とすること 人や社会のために何かしたことがある？	
お金になること 何かをしてお金をもらったことがある？	

Activity 9
ペアでシェアしよう Pair Share

Share your ideas with your partner using the writings from the previous activity.

例）**A:** 今まで、何かに夢中になったことがありますか。

B: はい。野球に夢中になったことがあります。

______________さんのこと

好きなこと 何かに夢中になったことがある？	
得意なこと 自信を持ってできることは何？	
世界が必要とすること 人や社会のために何かしたことがある？	
お金になること 何かをしてお金をもらったことがある？	

Activity 10
まとめてみよう Organize Discussion

Organize your discussion with your partner in Japanese.

Activity 11 ディスカッションしよう Group Discussion

Discuss the topic in groups in Japanese. Use the graphic organizer to capture members' ideas, opinions, and feelings. As you listen to members' ideas, jot down key information in the graphic organizer. Finally, write down the commonalities in the middle section.

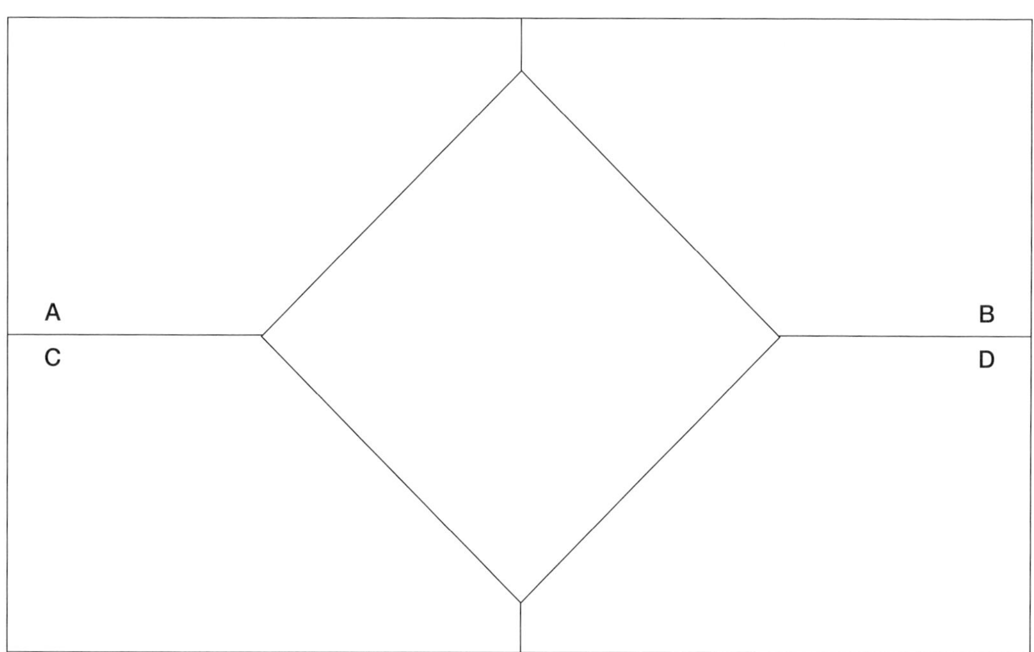

Activity 12 すらすら読(よ)もう Read Fluently

Read the article (Activity 3) to your partner. Pay attention to pronunciation, intonation, and tempo as you read aloud.

Activity 13 要約(ようやく)しよう Let's Summarize!

Summarize the article(s) in Japanese.

日本語でやってみよう Let's Show What We Can Do!

私の生きがい探し My *Ikigai* Search (Reflection)

Now that you have learned about the four elements of *ikigai*, write a reflection on your life experiences based on the four elements in order to share your *Ikigai* at a seminar in Japan.

Required

☐ ～たことがあります。

Optional

☐ 私の意見では、～
☐ ～と思います。
☐ まず／最初に、～
☐ 次に、～

Unit 6
Lesson 1

Learning Cycle 2

生き(い)がいを感(かん)じていること

My *Ikigai*

Have you ever immersed yourself in doing something and lost sense of time? Some researchers call this "state of flow" and the science explains that this "flow" is when people feel the most joy. In this learning cycle, first you will recall the occasions when you felt such flow moments. Then, explore possible reasons for such experiences in groups. Finally, you will pitch a plan for your passion project to inspire others who share similar interests in Japan.

0 考えてみよう Let's Explore!

What ideas come to your mind when you think about the topic? Jot down keywords in Japanese below.

興味(きょうみ)があること

1 探ってみよう Investigate the World

Activity 1 文化の窓 Take a Look into Japanese Culture

Listen to Sensei's presentation twice. First, take notes on general ideas in English. When you listen a second time, jot down keywords in Japanese.

生きがいを感じていること My *Ikigai*

What is this information about?	
Keywords in Japanese	

Activity 2 まとめてみよう Graphic Organizer

Demonstrate your understanding of the previous presentation by organizing your ideas below.

2 いろいろな視点を学ぼう Recognize Diverse Perspectives

Activity 3 読んで学ぼう Read and Learn

1 読んでみよう Let's Read!

Read and annotate the article below. Then, answer the following comprehension questions.

生きがいを感じていること My *Ikigai*

22

まりさん（17歳）

　私が住んでいる町には、貧困で苦しんでいる子どもたちを助けるために、「子ども食堂」という場所があります。放課後、子どもたちが一緒に宿題をしたり、ご飯を食べたり、ゲームをしたりします。私は高校生になって、子ども食堂のボランティアに参加するようになりました。そこに来る子どもたちのために、役に立ちたいと思ったからです。

　ボランティア活動はつかれますが、終わった後に、「ありがとう」という言葉をかけてもらうと、またがんばろうという気持ちになります。私はこのボランティアを通して、一人ではできないことも、地域の人たちと協力し合えば、乗り越えられるということを学びました。将来は、日本だけでなく、海外のボランティア活動にも参加してみたいと思っています。そのために、今、語学の勉強もがんばっています。

翔さん（20歳）

　私はあまり読書が好きなほうではありませんでした。でも、今は１年で100冊ぐらい読むようになりました。高校に入って、友だちが自分の意見をみんなの前でしっかり話しているのを見て、私もそうなりたいと思ったのです。読書をすると、いろいろな知識や情報が入ってきます。でも、ただ読んでいるだけでは、自分の意見が言えるようにはなりません。自分の意見が言えるようになるために、疑問を持ちながら読むことにしています。また、物事をいろいろな面から考えられるようになるために、疑問に思ったことは必ず調べることにしています。このような習慣は、将来にも役立つと思います。

1) What was Mari's motivation for volunteering for this organization?

2) What are some takeaways from her experiences through volunteering at this location?

3) What is Mari's plan for the future?

4) What motivated Sho to become an avid reader?

5) According to Sho, what is the habit that will help him in the future?

ことばリスト 

□放課後　□役に立つ　□ボランティア活動　□（言葉を）かける　□気持ち　□協力し合う　□乗り越える

□語学　□読書　□知識　□疑問（を持つ／に思う）　□物事　□いろいろな面　□習慣

2 空欄に入れよう Filling in the Blanks/Chart

Fill in the blank/chart with the appropriate keywords.

動機／目的	活動／学び
例）貧困で苦しんでいる子どもたちを助けるために	「子ども食堂」という場所がある。
1)「子ども食堂」に来る子どもたちのために	
2) 将来、海外のボランティア活動に参加するために	
3) 自分の意見が言えるようになるために	
4) 物事をいろいろな面から考えられるようになるために	

Activity 4 ペアでシェアしよう Pair Share

Share your understanding from the previous activities with your partner.

例）まりさんは、「子ども食堂」に来る子どもたちのために、役に立ちたいと思っています。

Activity 5 グループでシェアしよう Group Share

Converse with your group members about the topic in Japanese.

例）まりさんは、「子ども食堂」に来る子どもたちのために、役に立ちたいと思っています。

Activity 6

質問に答えよう Respond to the Questions

Answer the following questions based on what you have read about the topic.

例)「子ども食堂」は、だれのためにありますか。

貧困で苦しんでいる子どもたちのためにあります。

1) まりさんは、何のために語学の勉強をがんばっていますか。

2) 翔さんは、何のために本を読むことにしていますか。

3 アイデアを交換しよう Communicate Ideas

Activity 7

文法パターンを見つけよう Let's Explore Language Structure!

1 聞いてみよう Let's Listen!

PPT

Listen to Sensei's presentation and jot down key ideas.

2 新しい文法パターンは？ Where is a New Language Structure?

What is the common language structure? Highlight below.

- 貧困で苦しんでいる子どもたちを助けるために、「子ども食堂」という場所があります。
- 将来、海外のボランティア活動に参加するために、語学の勉強もがんばっています。
- 自分の意見が言えるようになるために、疑問を持ちながら読むことにしています。

3 意味は？ What Could It Mean?

Discuss possible meanings of the language structure as a class.

4 使い方は？ How Can We Use It?

Discuss possible ways to use the language structure as a class.

5 使ってみよう Let's Use the New Language Structure!

Use the language structure in new situations.

目的	していること
例）自分の意見が言えるようになるために	本を100冊読むことにしました。
1) ______	ボランティア活動に参加しています。
2) ______	毎日、外国語の勉強をしています。
3) ______	

Activity 8 書いてみよう Write It Out

Express your ideas in writing using the new language structure.

私が取り組みたいこと

動機／目的	活動／学び
例）貧困で苦しんでいる人を助けるために	フードバンクでボランティアをしたいです。
1.	
2.	
3.	
4.	

ペアでシェアしよう Pair Share

Share your ideas with your partner using the writings from the previous activity.

例) A: ○○さんは、これから、どんなことに取り組みたいですか。

B: 貧困で苦しんでいる人を助けるために、フードバンクでボランティアをしたいです。

__________さんが取り組みたいこと

動機／目的	活動／学び
例) 貧困で苦しんでいる人を助けるために	フードバンクでボランティアをしたいです。
1.	
2.	
3.	
4.	

Activity 10

まとめてみよう Organize Discussion

Organize your discussion with your partner in Japanese.

Activity 11

ディスカッションしよう Group Discussion

Discuss the topic in groups in Japanese. Use the graphic organizer to capture members' ideas, opinions, and feelings. As you listen to members' ideas, jot down key information in the graphic organizer. Finally, write down the commonalities in the middle section.

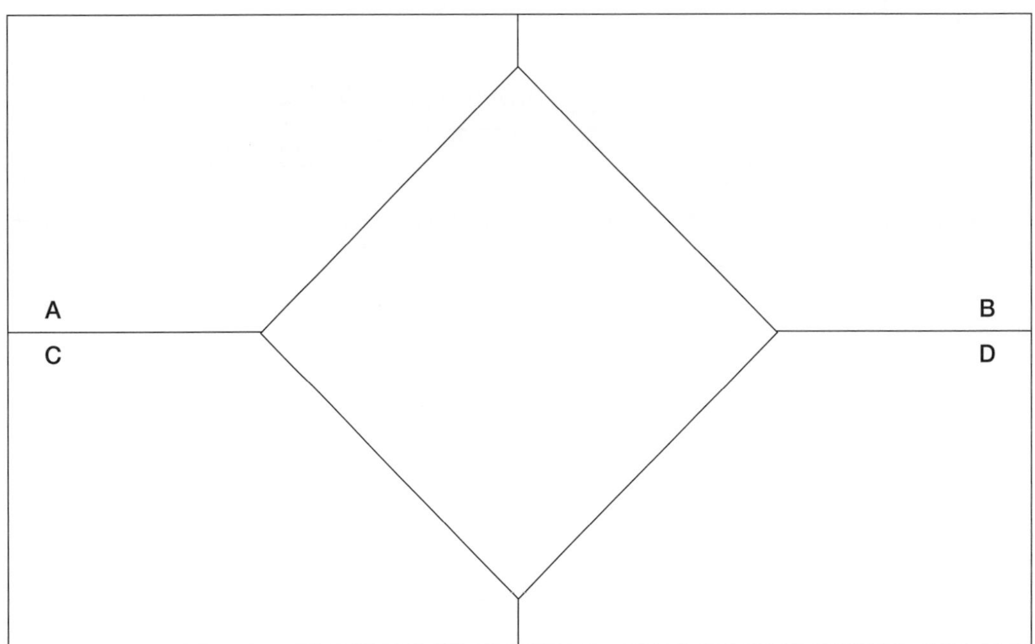

Activity 12

すらすら読(よ)もう Read Fluently

Read the article (Activity 3) to your partner. Pay attention to pronunciation, intonation, and tempo as you read aloud.

Activity 13

要約(ようやく)しよう Let's Summarize!

Summarize the article(s) in Japanese.

4 日本語でやってみよう Let's Show What We Can Do!

これから取り組みたいこと

My Contribution to the Community (Essay)

You have learned about "State of Flow" and possible reasons for such experiences. Write and post a short essay about things that you feel passionate about and how they could help your community in order to inspire Japanese high school students.

Required

- ☐ ～ために、～
- ☐ ～たいと思います。

Optional

- ☐ 私の意見では、～
- ☐ ～ので、～
- ☐ まず／最初に、～
- ☐ 次に、～

Unit 6 Mid Task

日本語でアクション！

Take Action in Japanese!

情熱プロジェクト My Passion Project (Sales Pitch)

What passion and skills do you bring to the world? Pitch a plan for your passion project to inspire others who share similar interests in Japan. Your pitch must include your passion, experience, skill sets you have or interest in developing, and lastly invite others to join your cause.

Unit 6 未来へのコンパス Compass to My Future

How can we live our lives meaningfully?

Lesson 2 よりよい社会 Better Future World

Essential Questions:

- What are some ways we can make positive influences in the ever-changing world?
- What can we bring to the world both individually and collectively?
- What can we do to prepare for a rich and fulfilling life in the future?

Can-do List:

Check!

- ☐ Describe what kind of person I want to be and why
- ☐ Explain what I can do to contribute to the world

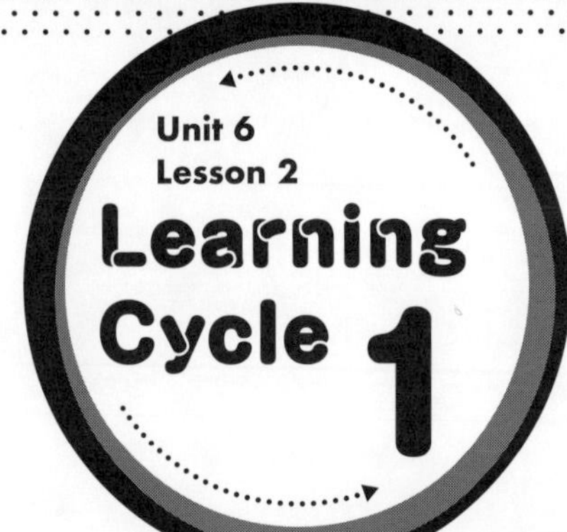

世界のために私たちができること

Things We Can Do to Make the World a Better Place

What can one do to prepare for a rich and fulfilling life in the future? Are there any ways we can make positive influences in the ever-changing world? In this learning cycle, you will explore the Sustainable Development Goals (SDGs) and learn about the areas of improvement. Then, you will identify an area that resonates the most with you. Finally, you will draft and give a “sales pitch” in promoting the SDG area of your choice to donors.

0 考えてみよう Let's Explore!

What do you notice in the title picture? (p.233) What ideas come to your mind when you think about the topic? Jot down keywords in Japanese below.

私にとって大切なこと

1 探ってみよう Investigate the World

Take a Look into Japanese Culture

PPT

Listen to Sensei’s presentation twice. First, take notes on general ideas in English. When you listen a second time, jot down keywords in Japanese.

世界のために私たちができること Things We Can Do to Make the World a Better Place

What is this information about?	
Keywords in Japanese	

Activity 2

まとめてみよう Graphic Organizer

Demonstrate your understanding of the previous presentation by organizing your ideas below.

2 いろいろな視点を学ぼう Recognize Diverse Perspectives

読んで学ぼう Read and Learn

1 読んでみよう Let's Read!

Read and annotate the article below. Then, answer the following comprehension questions.

世界のために私たちができること

Things We Can Do to Make the World a Better Place

世界には貧困、戦争、環境問題、病気など、さまざまな問題があります。これらの問題を解決し、私たちがこの地球に暮らし続けられるように、17の持続可能な開発目標(Sustainable Development Goals; SDGs)が立てられました。SDGsは、世界193か国で取り組んでいて、2030年までに達成されるべき目標とされています。私たちが生きていくためには、環境を守りながら、さまざまな社会活動、経済活動をしていく必要があります。SDGsの17の目標を3つのカテゴリーに分けると、次のようになります。
せかい　　ひんこん　せんそう　かんきょうもんだい　びょうき
きゅう　く　　　つづ　　　　　　　　　　　　　　じぞくかのう　かいはつもくひょう

環境カテゴリー

6. 安全な水とトイレを世界中に
13. 気候変動に具体的な対策を きこうへんどう ぐたいてき たいさく
14. 海の豊かさを守ろう うみ ゆた　　まも
15. 陸の豊かさも守ろう りく ゆた　　まも

私たちが住む地球を守るために、自然資源*を管理・節約したり、気候変動*の原因に対して対策を立てたりします。例えば、みんながきれいな水が飲めるように、海や川を汚さないようにします。また、地球温暖化*の原因となる二酸化炭素
わたし　　す　ちきゅう　まも　　　　　しぜんしげん　かんり　せつやく
きこうへんどう　げんいん　たい　たいさく　た　　　　　たと
みず　の　　　　　　うみ　かわ　よご
ちきゅうおんだんか　げんいん　　　　にさんかたんそ

1) What is the purpose of SDGs?

2) What are the three major categories of SDGs?

3) What suggestions are made in order to have clean water?

（CO_2）の量を減らすために、できるだけプラスチック製品を使わないようにします。

社会カテゴリー

1. 貧困をなくそう　　2. 飢餓をゼロに
3. すべての人に健康と福祉を　　4. 質の高い教育をみんなに
5. ジェンダー平等を実現しよう
7. エネルギーをみんなに、そしてクリーンに
11. 住み続けられるまちづくりを
16. 平和と公正をすべての人に

毎日、だれもが安心して安全に暮らせるように、人権を尊重し、平等な社会を目指します。例えば、ジェンダーに関係なく仕事ができるようにします。また、だれもが教育が受けられるようにします。

経済カテゴリー

8. 働きがいも経済成長も　　9. 産業と技術革新の基盤をつくろう
10. 人や国の不平等をなくそう　　12. つくる責任、つかう責任

私たちが充実した生活が送れるように、経済や社会や技術の発展に努力します。例えば、だれもが住みやすい街をつくるようにします。また、ものを作るときにゴミが出ないようにします。

これらの目標を達成するために必要なのは「**17.** パートナーシップで目標を達成しよう」です。私たちの世界が持続できるように、全ての国がパートナーとなって、また、そこに住む一人ひとりがSDGsを考えて行動することが大切です。

* **自然資源** natural resources、**気候変動** climate change、**地球温暖化** global warming

4) What are some sustainable goals in the Social category?

5) What are some sustainable goals in the Economy category?

6) According to the article, what is the one thing we must do to accomplish the goals?

ことばリスト 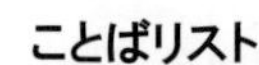

☐環境問題　☐（問題を）解決する　☐地球　☐暮らし続ける　☐（目標を）立てる　☐取り組む　☐達成する
☐目標　☐（環境を）守る　☐管理する　☐節約する　☐原因　☐対策　☐汚す　☐プラスチック製品
☐安心する　☐人権　☐充実する　☐（生活を）送る　☐発展　☐努力する　☐持続する

2 チェックリスト Checklist

Check off the keywords that apply to the information presented above.

行動	環境	社会	経済
例）ものを作るときにゴミが出ないようにする。	✓		✓
1) 海や川を汚さないようにする。			
2) プラスチック製品を使わないようにする。			
3) ジェンダーに関係なく仕事ができるようにする。			
4) だれもが教育が受けられるようにする。			
5) だれもが住みやすい街をつくるようにする。			
7) 男性と女性の給料を平等にするようにする。			
8) だれもがお金が借りられるようにする。			
9) バスや電車を利用するようにする。			

Activity 4
ペアでシェアしよう　Pair Share

Share your understanding from the previous activities with your partner.

例）環境のために、ものを作るときにゴミが出ないようにするべきだと思います。

Activity 5
グループでシェアしよう　Group Share

Converse with your group members about the topic in Japanese.

例）環境のために、ものを作るときにゴミが出ないようにするべきだと思います。

Activity 6
質問に答えよう　Respond to the Questions

Answer the following questions by referring to future actions.

例）環境のために、できることは何ですか。

ものを作るときに、できるだけゴミが出ないようにします。

1）環境のために、できることは何ですか。

2）社会のために、できることは何ですか。

3）経済のために、できることは何ですか。

3 アイデアを交換しよう　Communicate Ideas

Activity 7
文法パターンを見つけよう　Let's Explore Language Structure!

1 聞いてみよう Let's Listen!

Listen to Sensei's presentation and jot down key ideas.

2 新しい文法パターンは？ Where is a New Language Structure?

What is the common language structure? Highlight below.

- 海や川を汚さないようにします。
- できるだけプラスチック製品を使わないようにします。
- ものを作るときにゴミが出ないようにします。

3 意味は？ What Could It Mean?

Discuss possible meanings of the language structure as a class.

4 使い方は？ How Can We Use It?

Discuss possible ways to use the language structure as a class.

5 使ってみよう Let's Use the New Language Structure!

Use the language structure in new situations.

例）健康になりたい！

➡ 健康になるために、野菜を食べるようにします。

1）友だちをたくさん作りたい！

➡ ....

2）幸せになりたい！

➡ ....

3）＿＿＿＿＿＿＿＿＿＿＿＿！

➡ ....

Activity 8
書いてみよう Write It Out

Express your ideas in writing using the new language structure.

私にできること

目標	行動
例）二酸化炭素（CO_2）を減らすために	できるだけ自転車に乗るようにします。
1.	
2.	
3.	

Activity 9
ペアでシェアしよう Pair Share

Share your ideas with your partner using the writings from the previous activity.

例）A：よりよい世界にするために、できることを教えてください。
B：二酸化炭素（CO_2）を減らすために、できるだけ自転車に乗るようにします。

__________さんにできること

目標	行動
例）二酸化炭素（CO_2）を減らすために	できるだけ自転車に乗るようにします。
1.	
2.	
3.	

Activity 10
まとめてみよう Organize Discussion

Organize your discussion with your partner in Japanese.

Activity 11
ディスカッションしよう Group Discussion

Discuss the topic in groups in Japanese. Use the graphic organizer to capture members' ideas, opinions, and feelings. As you listen to members' ideas, jot down key information in the graphic organizer. Finally, write down the commonalities in the middle section.

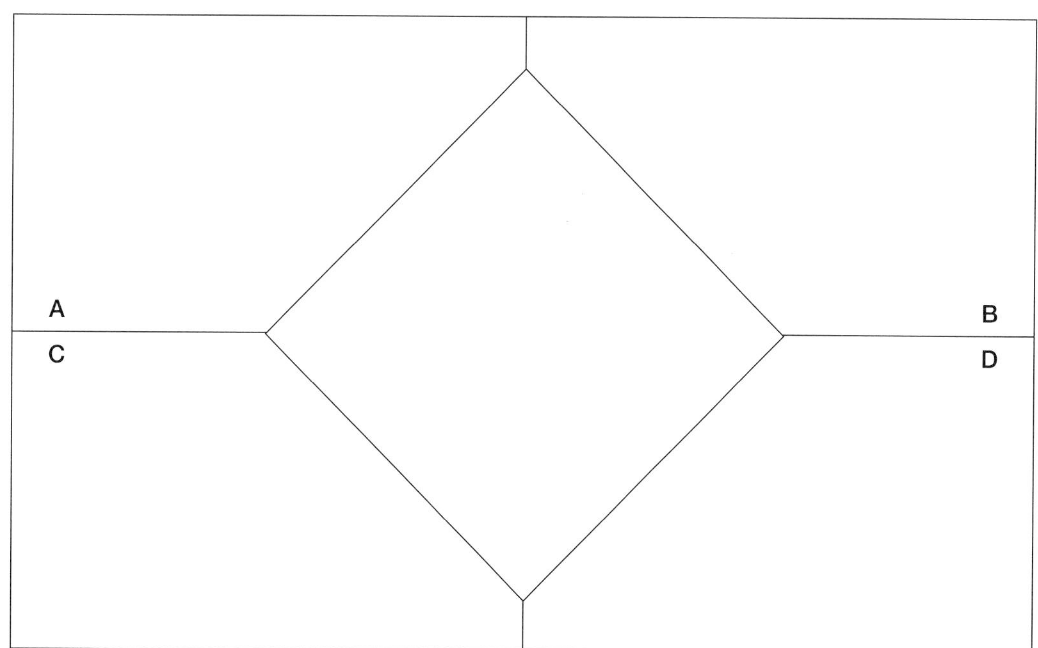

Activity 12
すらすら読(よ)もう Read Fluently

Read the article (Activity 3) to your partner. Pay attention to pronunciation, intonation, and tempo as you read aloud.

Activity 13 要約しよう Let's Summarize!

Summarize the article(s) in Japanese.

4 日本語でやってみよう Let's Show What We Can Do!

SDGs 目標達成への提案

Proposition to Attain Sustianable Development Goals (Short Speech)

You have learned about the SDGs and identify an area that resonates the most with you. Write and give a short sales pitch to promote your idea to make a positive influence in the chosen SDG category to a potential donor in Japan. Your speech must have a compelling reason for such change.

Required

- □ ～ために、～
- □ ～ようにします。

Optional

- □ 例えば、～
- □ ～なければなりません。
- □ まず／最初に、～
- □ 次に、～

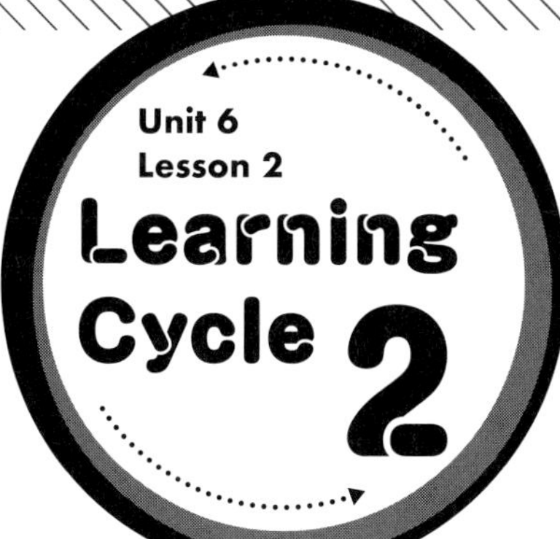

社会への私の願い

しゃかい わたし ねが

My Wishes for a Better Future

Everyone brings a gift to the world. *What is your gift to the world?* In this learning cycle, you will learn the complexity of one's identity through Japanese students' personal journeys. Then, you will identify the area(s) where your talent and/or passion can support making a difference in the world. Finally, you will write a future plan describing your values, passion, things you want to learn, and how you plan to apply your learning for the future.

0 考えてみよう Let's Explore!

What ideas come to your mind when you think about the topic? Jot down keywords in Japanese below.

将来の夢

しょうらい ゆめ

1 探ってみよう Investigate the World

Activity 1 文化の窓 Take a Look into Japanese Culture

Listen to Sensei's presentation twice. First, take notes on general ideas in English. When you listen a second time, jot down keywords in Japanese.

社会への私の願い My Wishes for a Better Future

What is this information about?	
Keywords in Japanese	

Activity 2 まとめてみよう Graphic Organizer

Demonstrate your understanding of the previous presentation by organizing your ideas below.

2 いろいろな視点を学ぼう Recognize Diverse Perspectives

Activity 3 読んで学ぼう Read and Learn

1 読んでみよう Let's Read!

Read and annotate the article below. Then, answer the following comprehension questions.

社会への私の願い My Wishes for a Better Future

24

子どものころ、よく私は「男の子」と間違われた。かっこいいヒーローものが好きで、いつも男の子と遊んでいたので、家族からも「女の子らしくしなさい」と言われた。それが嫌だった。

小学生のとき、クラスの劇で主人公になりたかったが、先生から「その役は男の子だから」と言われた。中学校の制服もとても違和感があった。本当はズボンをはきたかったが、校則で決められていたので、仕方なくスカートをはくことにした。

高校生になってから、「LGBTQ＋」という性的マイノリティの存在を知って、いろいろな記事を読むことにした。そして、やっと本当の自分を見つけることができた。もし、学校に「大丈夫だよ」「人の言うことは気にしなくていい」と味方になってくれる人がいたら、安心だと思った。だから、学校で「LGBTQ＋」について考えるクラブを作ることにした。

卒業後も、クラブの経験を活かして、ボランティア活動に参加したり、イベントを計画したりしたい。これからも、だれもがありのままで生きられる社会を目指して、いろいろな活動をしていきたい。家族からも理解されず、苦しんで悩んでいる人の力になれるように、努力をしたいと思う。

日本の社会ではまだまだ「女の子は女の子らしく」「男の子は男の子らしく」が常識となっている。しかし、人間は一人ひとり違うから、自分の価値観を押し付けることは偏見や差別につながり、人を傷つけると思う。お互いありのままを受け入れ、支え合い、理解し合いながら、生きられる社会になることが私の願いだ。

1) What was the common public perception about the author growing up?

2) What prompted the author to start a LGBTQ+ club?

3) What does the author plan to do in the future?

4) Which SDG category does this issue best fit in?

ことばリスト 

□願い □間違う □ヒーローもの □～らしい □劇 □主人公 □役 □制服 □違和感(がある)
□校則 □仕方ない □性的マイノリティ □存在 □記事 □やっと □気にする □味方(になる)
□安心 □計画する □ありのまま □苦しむ □力になる □まだまだ □常識(となる)
□(価値観を)押し付ける □偏見 □差別 □(差別に)つながる □(人を)傷つける □理解し合う

2 チェックリスト　Checklist

Check off the keywords that apply to the information presented above.

	経験したこと	思ったこと
例）家族から「女の子らしくしなさい」と言われた。	✓	
1) 仕方なくスカートをはくことにした。		
2) 先生から「その役は男の子だから」と言われた。		
3) 味方になってくれる人がいたら、安心だと思った。		
4) だれもがありのままで生きられる社会を目指して、いろいろな活動をしていきたい。		
5) ありのままを受け入れ、理解し合いながら、生きられる社会になる。		

Activity 4

ペアでシェアしよう　Pair Share

Share your understanding from the previous activities with your partner.

例）筆者は、子どものころ、家族から「女の子らしくしなさい」と言われたことがあります。

Activity 5

グループでシェアしよう　Group Share

Converse with your group members about the topic in Japanese.

例）筆者は、子どものころ、家族から「女の子らしくしなさい」と言われたことがあります。

Activity 6
質問に答えよう　Respond to the Questions

Answer the following questions based on what you have read about the topic.

例）筆者は、校則を守るために、どうしましたか。
仕方なくスカートをはくことにしました。

1）筆者は、性的マイノリティの存在を知って、どうしましたか。

2）筆者は、味方になってくれる人がいたら安心だと思って、どうしましたか。

3 アイデアを交換しよう　Communicate Ideas

Activity 7
文法パターンを見つけよう　Let's Explore Language Structure!

1 聞いてみよう　Let's Listen!

PPT

Listen to Sensei's presentation and jot down key ideas.

2 新しい文法パターンは？　Where is a New Language Structure?

What is the common language structure? Highlight below.

- 校則で決められていたので、仕方なくスカートをはくことにした。
- いろいろな記事を読むことにした。
- 学校で「LGBTQ+」について考えるクラブを作ることにした。

3 意味は？　What Could It Mean?

Discuss possible meanings of the language structure as a class.

4 使い方は？ How Can We Use It?

Discuss possible ways to use the language structure as a class.

5 使ってみよう Let's Use the New Language Structure!

Use the language structure in new situations.

例）（性的マイノリティのために）➡ クラブを作ることにします。

1）（家族のために）

➡ ……………………

2）（友だちのために）

➡ ……………………

3）（社会のために）

➡ ……………………

4）（＿＿＿＿＿＿のために）

➡ ……………………

Activity 8 書いてみよう Write It Out

Express your ideas in writing using the new language structure.

私の経験から決心したこと

経験したこと	決心したこと
	• • •

Activity 9
ペアでシェアしよう Pair Share

Share your ideas with your partner using the writings from the previous activity.

例) A: 経験から決心したことを教えてください。

B: 私は高校生になって、「LGBTQ+」という性的マイノリティの存在を知りました。その経験から、「LGBTQ+」について考えるクラブを作ることにしました。

＿＿＿＿さんの経験から決心したこと

経験したこと	決心したこと
	• • •

Activity 10
まとめてみよう Organize Discussion

Organize your discussion with your partner in Japanese.

Activity 11 ディスカッションしよう Group Discussion

Discuss the topic in groups in Japanese. Use the graphic organizer to capture members' ideas, opinions, and feelings. As you listen to members' ideas, jot down key information in the graphic organizer. Finally, write down the commonalities in the middle section.

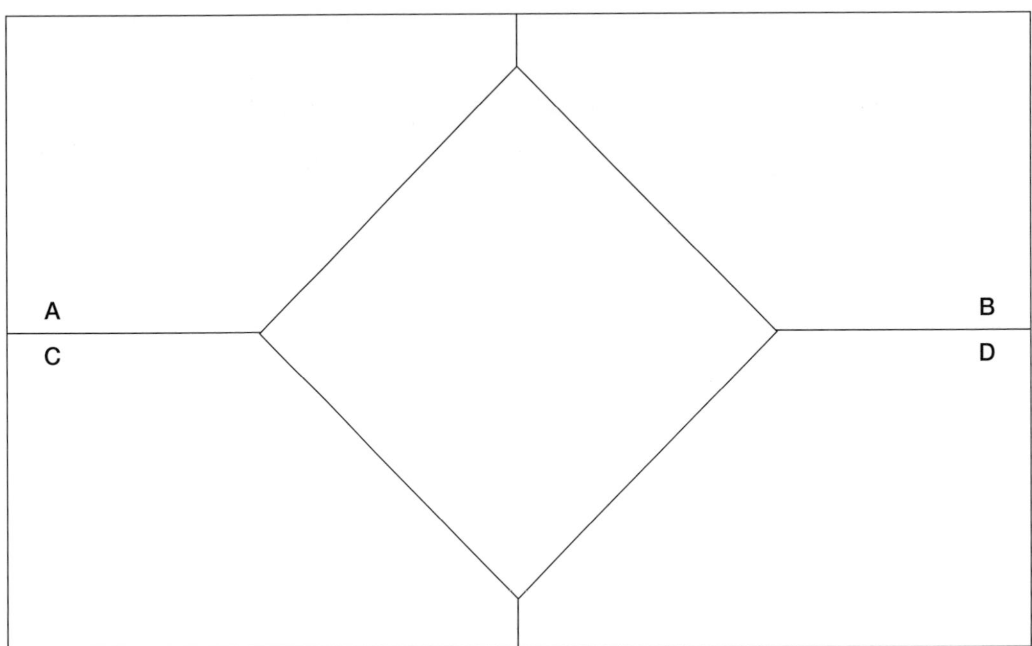

Activity 12 すらすら読もう Read Fluently

Read the article (Activity 3) to your partner. Pay attention to pronunciation, intonation, and tempo as you read aloud.

Activity 13 要約しよう Let's Summarize!

Summarize the article(s) in Japanese.

4 日本語でやってみよう Let's Show What We Can Do!

私の未来への願い My Wishes for the Future (Presentaion)

Now that you indentify the areas where your talent and passion can support making a difference in the world. You are invited to make a speech for Japanese speech contest. Write a short speech where you address the issues that are pressing to your generation and your recommendations for it. Begin your speech with the issue, why it's important to you, and finally your wishes for positive changes.

スピーチの流れ	質問	答え
書き出し	・あなたにとって、今、大切なことは何？ ・社会にとって、今、大切なことは何だと思う？	
経験	どんな経験をしたことがある？ ・つらかった経験 ・一人ぼっちの経験 ・いじめを見た／いじめられた経験 ・人を助けた／人に助けられた経験	
経験から決心したこと	・学校／社会をどう変えたい？ ・何をすることにする？	

Unit 6 Final Task

日本語でアクション！

Take Action in Japanese!

未来(みらい)へのコンパス My Future Pathway Plan

Task Sheet & Rublics 

Congratulations! You have learned about yourself and others through Japanese studies. You must be proud of your accomplishments. Now, as a final project, write a future plan describing your values, passion, things you want to earn, and how you plan to apply your learning for the future. Your plan will be published along with your classmates' plans and shared with people around the world.

Your Role & Purpose	Students reflect on their experiences, and state contributions to the world after graduation
Your Audience	Japanese high school students, classmates, family
Language	☐ Reflection on experiences (1-2 important events) ☐ Describe personal characteristics/values/strengths ☐ Explain what *Ikigai* means to you ☐ Discuss your future goals/aspirations/passions ☐ Describe how you want to contribute to the world after high school
Product	**Product Type:** ☐ Hand-written, within the margins ☐ All text must be written in black ink **Optional:** ☐ Drawings/illustrations/decorations

Can-do List

Pause and reflect what you can do with Japanese at the end of each unit. Celebrate your accomplishments and notice how and what you can do better next time.

私たちの生活とテクノロジー
Technology and Our Lives

Targeted Proficiency: Intermediate Mid

INTERPRETIVE: Reading and Listening

Tasks	Yes, with confidence!	Yes, with little help.	Yes, with much help.	Not yet.
I can identify behaviors before and after smartphones by listening to a presentation.				
I can obtain key information on behaviors before and after smartphones by reading articles.				
I can identify popular apps among young people in Japan by listening to a presentation.				
I can obtain key information on popular apps among young people in Japan by reading articles.				
I can identify the negative effects of smartphone use by listening to a presentation.				
I can obtain key information on the negative effects of smartphone use by reading articles.				
I can identify the possible solutions for smartphone addiction by listening to a presentation.				
I can obtain key information on the possible solutions for smartphone addiction by reading articles.				

INTERPERSONAL MODE: Speaking and Writing

Tasks	Yes, with confidence!	Yes, with little help.	Yes, with much help.	Not yet.
I can discuss the benefits of smartphone functions with others.				
I can ask others about popular apps among Japanese young people and us.				

I can find out the negative effects of smartphone use from classmates.				
I can discuss methods to prevent overuse of smartphones.				

PRESENTATIONAL MODE: Speaking and Writing

Tasks	Yes, with confidence!	Yes, with little help.	Yes, with much help.	Not yet.
I can compare behaviors before and after smartphones.				
I can compare and describe popular smartphone apps in Japan and my country.				
I can give opinions about various apps and tech tools.				
I can give reasons as to why certain apps are popular.				
I can list typical characteristics of people who develop smartphone addiction.				
I can explain the effects of smartphone overuse.				
I can debate with classmates about the influence of smartphones.				
I can share my perspectives on smartphones with my classmates.				
I can propose possible prevention methods for overuse of smartphones.				

Unit 2 進化するデザイン Evolving Design

Targeted Proficiency: Intermediate Mid

INTERPRETIVE: Reading and Listening

Tasks	Yes, with confidence!	Yes, with little help.	Yes, with much help.	Not yet.
I can obtain key information on the functions and characteristics of Japanese products by listening to a presentation.				
I can obtain key information about the functions and characteristics of Japanese products by reading product descriptions.				
I can obtain key information on how to choose products by listening to a presentation.				
I can obtain key information about how to choose products by reading product descriptions.				
I can obtain key information on what makes good design by listening to a presentation.				
I can obtain key information about what makes good design by reading an article.				

INTERPERSONAL MODE: Speaking and Writing

Tasks	Yes, with confidence!	Yes, with little help.	Yes, with much help.	Not yet.
I can converse with others about characteristics and functions of various products.				
I can discuss the criteria of products with others.				
I can find out the designs that improve our lives with others.				

I can obtain information about others' criteria for "Good Design."				
I can recommend products to others based on good design criteria.				

PRESENTATIONAL MODE: Speaking and Writing

Tasks	Yes, with confidence!	Yes, with little help.	Yes, with much help.	Not yet.
I can describe characteristics and functions of various products.				
I can evaluate the products by using criteria and recommend the products that improve our lives.				
I can compare Japanese and your country's products and state my opinions.				
I can share things and/or services that are improving the lives of your community members.				
I can write a short article to bring awareness of the positive impact of good design on our society.				
I can share my perspectives on designs.				
I can introduce designs of existing everyday items to improve our lives as well as Japanese people's lives.				

Unit 3 日本芸術への響き
(にほんげいじゅつ ひび)
Be Inspired by Japanese Art

Targeted Proficiency: Intermediate Mid

INTERPRETIVE: Reading and Listening

Tasks	Yes, with confidence!	Yes, with little help.	Yes, with much help.	Not yet.
I can identify key information about traditional Japanese art forms by listening to a presentation.				
I can obtain key information about traditional Japanese art forms by reading articles.				
I can identify key information about art appreciation by listening to a presentation.				
I can identify a person's impression of an art piece by reading art appreciation writings.				

INTERPERSONAL MODE: Speaking and Writing

Tasks	Yes, with confidence!	Yes, with little help.	Yes, with much help.	Not yet.
I can ask others about their opinion and impressions on various woodblock prints.				
I can find out others' interpretations and impressions of various art pieces.				
I can share key points on how to draw ink paintings.				
I can discuss the roles of the host and guests in a Japanese tea ceremony.				

PRESENTATIONAL MODE: Speaking and Writing

Tasks	Yes, with confidence!	Yes, with little help.	Yes, with much help.	Not yet.
I can prepare and give a short presentation on a Japanese art form of my choice.				
I can write an art appreciation post on an art piece of my choice.				
I can describe my experience creating traditional ink paintings by writing a vlog post.				
I can compare the Japanese tea ceremony to a performing art form from my country through a compare and contrast article.				
I can share the cultural perspectives of Japanese woodblock prints, ink paintings, and tea ceremonies.				
I can design and create a piece of Japanese artwork to express the relationship between myself and Japan.				

Unit 4 成功を夢見て

Dream of Success

Targeted Proficiency: Intermediate Mid

INTERPRETIVE: Reading and Listening

Tasks	Yes, with confidence!	Yes, with little help.	Yes, with much help.	Not yet.
I can identify major events of Japanese immigrant and Japanese American history by listening to a presentation.				
I can obtain key information about Japanese immigrants and Japanese American by reading articles.				
I can identify key information about reasons for why people immigrate to other countries by listening to a presentation.				
I can identify various reasons for immigrating to another country by reading an article.				
I can obtain key information about immigrant families by listening to a presentation.				
I can identify key information about immigrant families who came to my city by reading their family stories.				

INTERPERSONAL MODE: Speaking and Writing

Tasks	Yes, with confidence!	Yes, with little help.	Yes, with much help.	Not yet.
I can discuss historical events of Japanese immigrants and Japanese American history.				
I can ask others what events resonated with them the most about immigrant family stories.				
I can find out what reasons a person would immigrate to another country for.				

I can find out others' family stories including key events, experiences, and feelings.				
I can converse with others about my own family's immigration story.				

PRESENTATIONAL MODE: Speaking and Writing

Tasks	Yes, with confidence!	Yes, with little help.	Yes, with much help.	Not yet.
I can describe the lifestyle of Japanese immigrants & Japanese Americans and give my opinion by writing a short summary.				
I can describe a personal immigration story of my choice by writing a summary.				
I can describe the lifestyle of Japanese immigrants & Japanese Americans and give my opinion by writing a cinquain poem.				
I can describe reasons for Japanese immigration and state my opinion and feelings towards such reasons.				
I can share my perspectives on immigration.				
I can share my family's immigration story by writing a piece for a story collection.				

Unit 5 ともに生きる社会 Diverse Society

Targeted Proficiency: Intermediate Mid

INTERPRETIVE: Reading and Listening

Tasks	Yes, with confidence!	Yes, with little help.	Yes, with much help.	Not yet.
I can obtain key information about the reasons foreigners live in Japan by listening to a presentation.				
I can obtain key information about the reasons foreigners live in Japan by reading articles.				
I can obtain key information about diversity in Japan by listening to a presentation.				
I can obtain key information about the growing diversity in Japan by reading articles.				
I can identify key information about identity and the racially mixed people's experience in Japan by listening to presentations.				
I can identify key information about identity and the racially mixed people's experience in Japan by reading articles.				

INTERPERSONAL MODE: Speaking and Writing

Tasks	Yes, with confidence!	Yes, with little help.	Yes, with much help.	Not yet.
I can discuss reasons for why more foreigners are moving to Japan.				
I can discuss the benefits and challenges of having diversity.				
I can ask others about their opinions on the racially mixed people's experiences in Japan.				

I can converse with others about my own identity.				
I can interview others on key information about their identity.				

PRESENTATIONAL MODE: Speaking and Writing

Tasks	Yes, with confidence!	Yes, with little help.	Yes, with much help.	Not yet.
I can describe reasons for foreigners moving to Japan by writing a short summary.				
I can describe the benefits and challenges of having diversity by writing a short article.				
I can write a news report to raise awareness on the increasing diversity in Japan.				
I can raise awareness about the discrimination and inequality racially mixed people experience in Japan by writing a short essay.				
I can describe my own identity by writing a poem.				
I can share my perspectives on identity.				
I can write a podcast episode on the topic of identity.				

未来へのコンパス
Compass to My Future

Targeted Proficiency: Intermediate Mid

INTERPRETIVE: Reading and Listening

Tasks	Yes, with confidence!	Yes, with little help.	Yes, with much help.	Not yet.
I can identify key information about the concept of *Ikigai* by listening to a presentation.				
I can obtain key information about the concept of *Ikigai* by reading an article.				
I can identify things a person is passionate about by listening to a presentation.				
I can identify things a person is passionate about by reading an article.				
I can identify key information about the "SDGs" by listening to a presentation.				
I can obtain key information about the "SDGs" by reading an article.				
I can identify key information about one's life plan and wish by listening to a presentation.				
I can identify key information about one's life plan and wish by reading an article.				

INTERPERSONAL MODE: Speaking and Writing

Tasks	Yes, with confidence!	Yes, with little help.	Yes, with much help.	Not yet.
I can ask others about their *Ikigai*.				
I can ask others about things they are passionate about and their future plans.				

I can discuss how I and others can contribute to the world.				
I can ask others about their life experiences, plans and wishes.				
I can share with others about my life experiences, plans, and wishes.				

PRESENTATIONAL MODE: Speaking and Writing

Tasks	Yes, with confidence!	Yes, with little help.	Yes, with much help.	Not yet.
I can introduce my own *Ikigai* by writing a reflection.				
I can describe things I am passionate about and my future plans by writing a short essay.				
I can present my plan about things I am passionate about by creating a pitch.				
I can describe how I can contribute to the world by making a two minute speech on the chosen SDG category.				
I can describe my life experiences, plans, and wishes by writing a short speech.				
I can share my perspectives on contributions to the world.				
I can write a future plan describing my values, passion, things I want to earn, and how I plan to apply my learning for the future.				

VOCABULARY INDEX

あ

あい	愛	love	U4	L1	LC2
あいて	相手	the other person	U1	L1	LC1
あかり	明かり	light	U3	L1	LC2
あかるい(ひと)	明るい(人)	cheerful (person)	U5	L2	LC2
あくえいきょう	悪影響	bad influence, adverse effects	U1	L2	LC1
あこがれる	あこがれる	to attracted to, to dream	U5	L1	LC1
(えいきょうを)あたえる	(影響を)与える	to give (an effect/an influence)	U1	L2	LC1
(やすらぎを)あたえる	(安らぎを)与える	to give (a comfort)	U2	L2	LC1
あたためる	温める	to warm up	U2	L1	LC1
あつりょく	圧力	pressure	U2	L1	LC1
(たようせいを)あらわす	(多様性を)表す	to represent (diversity)	U5	L1	LC2
ありのまま	ありのまま	the way it is	U6	L2	LC2
ある～	ある～	a certain ～	U5	L1	LC1
(ちからを)あわせる	(力を)合わせる	to put (power/force) together	U4	L1	LC2
あんしん	安心	ease, peace of mind	U6	L2	LC2
あんしんする	安心する	to feel ease	U6	L2	LC1
あんぜん	安全	safe	U2	L1	LC2
あんていする	安定する	to be stable	U4	L2	LC2

い

いいかえる	言い換える	to paraphrase, to rephrase	U5	L2	LC1
(とくせいを)いかす	(特性を)活かす	to take advantage of (the characteristics of something)	U5	L1	LC2
いきもの	生き物	living creatures	U3	L1	LC1
～いこう	～以降	since ～, after ～ (time/period)	U4	L1	LC1
いごこち(のいい)	居心地(のいい)	cozy, comfortable	U3	L1	LC2
いじする	持続する	to continue	U6	L2	LC1
いじゅうする	移住する	to immigrate	U4	L1	LC1
～いじょう	～以上	more than ～	U2	L1	LC2
いぜん	以前	before, previously	U1	L1	LC1
いぞんしょう	依存症	addiction	U1	L2	LC1
いちぶ	一部	part of	U5	L1	LC2
いつか	いつか	someday	U5	L2	LC2
いっしょに	一緒に	together	U2	L2	LC1
いっぱんてき	一般的	generally, typically	U5	L2	LC1
いなか	田舎	country side	U4	L2	LC2
いばしょ	居場所	place to belong	U5	L2	LC1
いまにも	今にも	momentarily, soon after	U3	L1	LC1
いみん	移民	immigrants	U4	L1	LC1
いみんせいさく	移民政策	immigration policy	U4	L1	LC1
いや	嫌	unplesant, unpreferable	U5	L2	LC2
いろいろなめん	いろいろな面	many possibility	U6	L1	LC2
いわかん(がある)	違和感(がある)	(to have) uneased feeling	U6	L2	LC2
いんしょう(にのこる)	印象(に残る)	(to make) an impression	U3	L1	LC2

う

うけいれたいせい	受け入れ態勢	accepting condition	U5	L1	LC1
(ちがいを)うけいれる	(違いを)受け入れる	to accept (differences)	U5	L1	LC2
うけとめかた	受けとめ方	the way to accept	U5	L2	LC1
うけとめる	受けとめる	to accept	U5	L2	LC1
うけとる	受け取る	to recieve, to accept	U1	L1	LC2
(ひょうかを)うける	(評価を)受ける	to receive (an evaluation)	U2	L1	LC2
(きょういくを)うける	(教育を)受ける	to get (an education)	U4	L2	LC1
うごかす	動かす	to move	U3	L2	LC1
うすい	薄い	light (color)	U3	L2	LC1
うちこむ	打ち込む	to devote	U6	L1	LC1
うみだす	生み出す	to create	U5	L1	LC2

え

えいきょう	影響	influence, effect	U1	L2	LC1
えだ	枝	branch	U3	L2	LC1
えもじ	絵文字	emoji	U1	L1	LC2
えらぶ	選ぶ	to select, to chose	U1	L1	LC1
えんげき	演劇	play, performing art	U2	L2	LC1

お

おいたち	生い立ち	personal backbround	U4	L1	LC2
おおけが(をする)	大けが(をする)	(to get) injured badly	U4	L2	LC2
おきる	起きる	to happen	U4	L1	LC1
(メッセージを)おくる	(メッセージを)送る	to send (a message)	U1	L1	LC2
(しょうを)おくる	(賞を)贈る	to give (gift, prize, etc)	U2	L2	LC2
(せいかつを)おくる	(生活を)送る	to live (life)	U6	L2	LC1
(かみを)おさえる	(紙を)押さえる	to hold (paper)	U3	L2	LC1
おさない	幼い	child, infant, immature	U4	L2	LC2
(かちかんを)おしつける	(価値観を)押し付ける	to force (one's value)	U6	L2	LC2
おしゃべりする	おしゃべりする	to chat	U3	L1	LC2
おそなえもの	お供え物	offerings	U2	L2	LC1
おたがい	お互い	mutually	U4	L2	LC2
(こころを)おちつかせる	(心を)落ち着かせる	to calm (mind)	U3	L2	LC2
おちつく	落ち着く	to calm down, to feel calm	U1	L2	LC1
(しりょく／しこうりょくが)おちる	(視力／思考力が)落ちる	to decline, to get rusty (vision, ability to think)	U1	L2	LC1
(こいに)おちる	(恋に)落ちる	to fall in (love)	U4	L1	LC2
おと	音	sound	U3	L1	LC1
おとずれる	訪れる	to visit	U3	L1	LC2
おなじようなこと	同じようなこと	similar thing	U4	L1	LC1
おんど	温度	temperature, humidity	U2	L1	LC1

か

かいがい	海外	overseas	U4	L1	LC1
(もんだいを)かいけつする	(問題を)解決する	to solve (a problem)	U6	L2	LC1
がいこくじん	外国人	foreigner	U5	L1	LC1
がか	画家	painter, artists	U3	L1	LC1
かきはじめる	書き始める	to start to write	U5	L2	LC2
(えを)かく	(絵を)描く	to draw (picture)	U3	L1	LC1
かぐ	家具	furniture	U2	L2	LC2
(ふとんを)かける	(ふとんを)かける	to cover with (futon)	U2	L1	LC1
(ことばを)かける	(言葉を)かける	to say something	U6	L1	LC2
かこうする	加工する	to edit, to modify	U1	L1	LC2

かさなる	重なる	to coincide	U6	L1	LC1
かしこい	賢い	smart, wise	U1	L2	LC2
(せんが)かすれる	(線が)かすれる	to fade (a line)	U3	L2	LC1
(おかねを)かせぐ	(お金を)稼ぐ	to earn (money)	U5	L1	LC1
～がた	～型	~ model	U2	L2	LC1
かたち	形	shape	U2	L1	LC1
かたな	刀	sword	U3	L2	LC2
かち(がある)	価値(がある)	valuable, worth	U2	L1	LC2
かちかん(がかわる)	価値観(が変わる)	(to change) perspectives/values	U2	L2	LC2
かっき(のある)	活気(のある)	lively, vibrant	U4	L1	LC2
かつどう	活動	activity	U2	L2	LC1
かつやくする	活躍する	to play an active part	U3	L1	LC1
かつようする	活用する	to utilize	U5	L1	LC2
かてい	家庭	household	U2	L2	LC1
(ゆめを)かなえる	(夢を)かなえる	to make (dream) come true	U4	L2	LC1
かのうせい	可能性	possibility	U5	L1	LC2
かみ	紙	paper	U3	L1	LC1
かわっている	変わっている	strange, awkward	U5	L2	LC2
かわりに	代わりに	instead of	U1	L2	LC2
かんがえかた	考え方	the way of thinking	U4	L2	LC2
かんきょう	環境	environment	U2	L2	LC2
かんきょうもんだい	環境問題	environmental issues	U6	L2	LC1
かんけい	関係	relationship	U4	L1	LC2
かんけいない	関係ない	nothing to do with, unconcerned	U3	L2	LC2
かんこうきゃく	観光客	tourists	U3	L1	LC2
かんしゃする	感謝する	to appreciate, be thankful	U3	L2	LC2
(よろこびを)かんじる	(喜びを)感じる	to feel (happy)	U6	L1	LC1
かんそう	感想	reflection	U3	L1	LC2
かんちょう	館長	curator	U3	L1	LC2
かんりする	管理する	to manage	U6	L2	LC1

き

きが	飢餓	starvation	U4	L2	LC1
きかい	機会	opportunities	U1	L2	LC1
きがるに	気軽に	casually, without reserve	U1	L1	LC1
きぎょう	企業	company, coopration	U4	L2	LC1
きじ	記事	article	U6	L2	LC2
ぎしき	儀式	rituals	U3	L2	LC2
ぎじゅつ	技術	techinique, techonology	U5	L1	LC1
きじゅん	基準	standards、criteria, basis	U2	L1	LC2
(ひとを)きずつける	(人を)傷つける	to hurt (someone)	U6	L2	LC2
きたい	期待	expectation	U2	L1	LC2
きにいる	気に入る	to like, favorite	U1	L1	LC2
きにする	気にする	to pay attention	U6	L2	LC2
きになる	気になる	to be concerned	U1	L2	LC2
きのう	機能	function, features	U2	L1	LC1
きのうてき	機能的	functionable	U2	L1	LC2
きめる	決める	to decide	U1	L2	LC2
きもち	気持ち	feeling	U6	L1	LC2
ぎもん(をもつ／におもう)	疑問(を持つ／に思う)	to doubt	U6	L1	LC2
きゅうに	急に	suddenly	U4	L1	LC1
きょういく	教育	education	U4	L2	LC1
きょうみ(のある)	興味(のある)	(to have) an interest	U1	L1	LC2
きょうゆうする	共有する	to share	U1	L1	LC1
きょうりょくしあう	協力し合う	to support each other	U6	L1	LC2
きょだい	巨大	giant	U3	L1	LC1
(からだを)きよめる	(体を)清める	to purify (body)	U3	L2	LC2
きょり	距離	distance	U3	L2	LC2
きをつける	気をつける	to pay attention	U2	L1	LC1
きんしする	禁止する	to prohibit	U4	L1	LC1

く

くうかん	空間	space	U3	L2	LC1
くみあわせる	組み合わせる	to put together	U1	L1	LC2
くらしつづける	暮らし続ける	to continue living	U6	L2	LC1
くらす	暮らす	to live, to make living	U4	L1	LC2
くるしむ	苦しむ	to suffer	U6	L2	LC2
くろうする	苦労する	to have a hard time, have difficulty	U4	L1	LC2
～ぐん	～軍	(military) division	U4	L1	LC2
ぐんじん	軍人	military personel	U4	L1	LC2

け

けいかくする	計画する	to plan	U6	L2	LC2
けいけん	経験	experience	U4	L1	LC1
けいこうペン	蛍光ペン	highlighter	U2	L1	LC1
けいざいてき	経済的	economically, financially	U2	L2	LC1
げき	劇	a play	U6	L2	LC2
けす	消す	to erase	U2	L1	LC1
けっか	結果	results, outcome	U1	L2	LC1
けっこん	結婚	marriage	U4	L1	LC2
げんいん	原因	cause	U6	L2	LC1
けんこう	健康	health	U6	L1	LC1
げんざい	現在	present time, nowadays	U2	L1	LC1
～げんざい	～現在	as of ~	U4	L2	LC1
げんばく(＝げんしばくだん)	原爆(＝原子爆弾)	atomic bomb	U4	L1	LC1
けんり	権利	rights	U4	L2	LC1

こ

こい	濃い	deep/dark (color)	U3	L1	LC2
こい	恋	love	U4	L1	LC2
こうおん	高温	high temperature	U2	L1	LC1
こうかんする	交換する	to exchange	U1	L1	LC1
こうけんする	貢献する	to contribute	U6	L1	LC1
こうしゅうでんわ	公衆電話	public phone	U1	L1	LC1
(せいかつが)こうじょうする	(生活が)向上する	to improve (the quality of life)	U1	L1	LC1
こうそく	校則	school rules	U6	L2	LC2
こうどうする	行動する	to act, to make an action	U1	L2	LC1
こうふんする	興奮する	to be excited	U1	L2	LC1
こうれいしゃ	高齢者	elderly	U2	L2	LC1
(こっきょうを)こえる	(国境を)越える	to cross (the border)	U4	L1	LC2
(～まんにんを)こえる	(～万人を)超える	to exceed (a number of people)	U4	L2	LC1
ごがく	語学	language	U6	L1	LC2
こくさいけっこん	国際結婚	international marriage	U4	L1	LC2

こくせき	国籍	nationality	U4	L1	LC2
こころえ	心得	understanding, mindset	U3	L2	LC2
こさ	濃さ	darkness (color), depth in color	U3	L2	LC1
こざら	小皿	small plate	U3	L2	LC1
こそだて	子育て	child rearing	U6	L1	LC1
コツ	コツ	tip, technique	U3	L2	LC1
こっきょう	国境	national border	U4	L1	LC2
コミュニティ	コミュニティ	community	U6	L1	LC1
こんご	今後	form now on	U2	L2	LC1

さ

さいせんたん	最先端	cutting edge	U2	L2	LC2
さいのう(がある)	才能(がある)	(to have) a talent	U6	L1	LC1
さがす	探す	to search	U1	L1	LC2
(ふでの)さき	(筆の)先	tip of (the brush)	U3	L2	LC1
さぎょう(をする)	作業(をする)	(to do) a work	U2	L2	LC1
さくひん	作品	art piece	U3	L1	LC2
ささえあう	支え合う	to support each other, to rely on each other	U4	L2	LC2
さびしい	寂しい	lonely	U2	L2	LC1
さべつ	差別	descrimination	U6	L2	LC2
さほう	作法	etiquette	U3	L2	LC2
さまざま	さまざま	various	U2	L2	LC2
さんかする	参加する	to participate	U3	L2	LC2

し

し	詩	poem	U5	L2	LC2
しあわせ	幸せ	happiness	U4	L1	LC2
しかたない	仕方ない	can't be helped	U6	L2	LC2
じき	時期	timing, time	U4	L1	LC2
しこうりょく	思考力	cognitive power, ability to think	U1	L2	LC1
じこしょうかい	自己紹介	self introduction	U5	L2	LC2
しじん	詩人	poet	U5	L2	LC2
じしん	自信	confidence	U5	L1	LC2
しずけさ	静けさ	quietness	U3	L1	LC1
しぜん	自然	nature	U3	L1	LC1
じだい	時代	era, period of time	U1	L1	LC1
したじき	下敷き	desk pad	U3	L2	LC1
じつげん	実現	materialize	U5	L1	LC1
じっとみる	じっと見る	to stare	U3	L1	LC2
じどう	自動	automatic	U2	L1	LC1
じどり	自撮り	selfie	U1	L1	LC2
じまく	字幕	subtitles	U2	L2	LC1
しみんけん	市民権	citizenship	U4	L1	LC1
しや(がひろがる)	視野(が広がる)	(to widen)vision, field of view	U5	L1	LC2
しゃざいする	謝罪する	to apologize	U4	L1	LC1
～しゅう	～州	~ state	U4	L2	LC1
じゆう	自由	freedom	U4	L2	LC1
しゅうかん	習慣	custom, habit	U6	L1	LC2
しゅうきょう	宗教	religion	U4	L2	LC1
じゅうしする	重視する	to place empasis on	U2	L1	LC2
じゅうじつする	充実する	to fulfill	U6	L2	LC1
しゅうちゅうする	集中する	to focus	U1	L2	LC2
じゅうよう	重要	important	U2	L1	LC2
しゅじんこう	主人公	main character	U6	L2	LC2
しゅっしん	出身	hometown	U4	L1	LC2
しゅるい	種類	type, kind, variety	U2	L1	LC1
じゅんび	準備	preperation	U3	L2	LC1
しょう	賞	award	U2	L2	LC2
しょうがい(のある)	障害(のある)	(to have) disability	U5	L1	LC2
じょうきょう	状況	circumstances	U5	L2	LC1
しようじかん	使用時間	usage time	U1	L2	LC2
しょうじき	正直	honesty	U4	L2	LC2
じょうしき(となる)	常識(となる)	(to become) a common knowledge	U6	L2	LC2
しょうとつする	衝突する	to head on	U5	L1	LC2
じょうほう	情報	information	U1	L1	LC1
しょうらい	将来	future	U5	L2	LC2
しょくりょう	食料	foods	U4	L2	LC2
しょっき	食器	dishes	U3	L1	LC2
しょっく	ショック	shock	U5	L2	LC2
しらべる	調べる	to research	U1	L1	LC2
しられる	知られる	well known, famous	U5	L2	LC2
しりょく	視力	eye sight	U1	L2	LC1
じんけん	人権	human right	U6	L2	LC1
じんこう	人口	population	U4	L1	LC1
しんさ(する)	審査(する)	to judge	U2	L2	LC2
じんざい	人材	talented person	U5	L1	LC2
しんしつ	寝室	bedroom	U1	L2	LC2
じんしゅ	人種	race, ethnic group	U4	L1	LC2
しんせい	神聖	devine	U3	L2	LC2
じんぶつ	人物	characters	U3	L1	LC1

す

すいみんじかん	睡眠時間	sleeping time	U1	L2	LC1
すいみんぶそく	睡眠不足	lack of sleep	U1	L2	LC1
～すぎる	～すぎる	excessive	U1	L2	LC1
スキル(がある)	スキル(がある)	(to have) a skill	U6	L1	LC1
すくう	救う	to rescue	U5	L2	LC2
(きのうが)すぐれる	(機能が)優れる	outstanding (function)	U2	L1	LC1
(せいさくを)すすめる	(政策を)進める	to promote (a policy)	U4	L1	LC1
(にほんを)すすめる	(日本を)すすめる	to recommend (Japan)	U5	L1	LC1
すずり	すずり	suzuri (container for ink)	U3	L2	LC1
すみ	墨	ink	U3	L2	LC1
(はんがえを)する	(版画絵を)刷る	to print (a woodblock print)	U3	L1	LC1
(すみを)する	(墨を)する	to grind (an ink stick to make ink)	U3	L2	LC1

せ

せいかつ	生活	life, daily living	U1	L1	LC1
せいかつようひん	生活用品	daily necessities	U2	L1	LC1
～せいき	～世紀	~ century	U3	L1	LC2
せいこう	成功	success	U4	L2	LC1
せいてきマイノリティ	性的マイノリティ	sexual minority	U6	L2	LC2
せいひん	製品	products	U2	L1	LC1
せいふ	政府	government	U4	L1	LC1
せいふく	制服	uniform	U6	L2	LC2
せいべつ	性別	gender	U5	L1	LC2

(ほうりつが)せいりつする	(法律が)成立する	(law, policy) is established	U4	L1	LC1
せかい	世界	world	U6	L1	LC1
せかいじゅう	世界中	around the world	U4	L2	LC1
せきにん	責任	responsibility	U4	L2	LC2
せっきょくてき	積極的	actively, positively	U4	L1	LC1
せつやく(になる)	節約(になる)	(will) save	U2	L2	LC1
せつやくする	節約する	to save, be frugal	U6	L2	LC1
せまい	狭い	small space, narrow	U3	L2	LC2
せわ(をする)	世話(をする)	(to take) care	U4	L2	LC2
せん	線	line	U3	L2	LC1
せんご	戦後	post war	U4	L1	LC2
せんじゅうみん	先住民	indegenous people	U4	L2	LC1
せんそう	戦争	war	U4	L2	LC1
せんよう	専用	made for, to use ~ by	U1	L1	LC2

そ

そうぞうする	想像する	to imagine	U1	L1	LC1
そうぞうする	創造する	to create	U2	L2	LC2
そだてる	育てる	to raise (living thing)	U4	L2	LC2
そふ	祖父	grandfather	U4	L2	LC2
それぞれ	それぞれ	each, independently	U4	L2	LC2
そんざい	存在	exixtance	U6	L2	LC2
そんちょうする	尊重する	to respect	U5	L1	LC2

た

たいさく	対策	strategy	U6	L2	LC1
(~に)たいして	(~に)対して	against (something/someone)	U6	L1	LC1
たいしょう	対象	applicable, eligibility, target	U2	L2	LC2
だいどころようひん	台所用品	kitchenware	U2	L1	LC1
(ふでを)たおす	(筆を)倒す	to tilt (the brush)	U3	L2	LC1
たきわけ	炊き分け	different cooking mode	U2	L1	LC1
(ごはんを)たく	(ご飯を)炊く	to cook (rice)	U2	L1	LC1
たけ	竹	bamboo	U3	L2	LC1
たすかる	助かる	helpful	U2	L2	LC1
たすける	助ける	to help, to assist	U2	L2	LC1
たたみ	畳	tatami mats	U3	L2	LC2
だっこする	だっこする	to carry, to hug	U2	L2	LC1
たっせいする	達成する	to achieve	U6	L2	LC1
たてもの	建物	buildings	U2	L2	LC2
(ふでを)たてる	(筆を)立てる	to hold up (the brush)	U3	L2	LC1
(おちゃを)たてる	(お茶を)点てる	to make (a tea)	U3	L2	LC2
(もくひょうを)たてる	(目標を)立てる	to set (a goal)	U6	L2	LC1
たぶんかきょうせいしゃかい	多文化共生社会	mutualcultural society	U5	L1	LC1
ためす	試す	to try	U1	L2	LC2
たようせい	多様性	diversity	U5	L1	LC2
たような	多様な	diverse	U5	L1	LC2

ち

ちあん(がいい)	治安(がいい)	(good) public safety	U5	L1	LC1
ちいき	地域	area, region, surrounding area	U2	L2	LC1
ちから	力	power, force	U4	L1	LC2
ちからになる	力になる	to be helpful	U6	L2	LC2
ちきゅう	地球	earth	U6	L2	LC1
ちしき	知識	knowledge	U6	L1	LC2
ちず	地図	map	U1	L1	LC1
ちゅうい	注意	caution	U2	L1	LC1
ちゅうきんとう	中近東	Middle East	U4	L2	LC1
ちゅうしん	中心	center	U3	L1	LC2
ちゅうなんべい	中南米	Latin America	U4	L2	LC1
ちゅうもく(をあつめる)	注目(を集める)	(to draw) attention	U1	L1	LC2
ちょうきたいざいしゃ	長期滞在者	long term visitor	U5	L1	LC2
ちょうさ	調査	research	U5	L1	LC1
ちょうせいする	調整する	to adjust	U3	L2	LC1
ちょうせつする	調節する	to adjust	U2	L1	LC1
ちょうり	調理	cooking	U2	L1	LC1

つ

つうち	通知	notification	U1	L2	LC2
つうはん	通販	online shopping	U1	L1	LC2
(チャンスを)つかむ	(チャンスを)つかむ	to grab (a chance)	U4	L2	LC1
つきあいかた	付き合い方	how to interact	U1	L2	LC2
(きのうが)つく	(機能が)付く	provided (function)	U2	L1	LC1
つくりあげる	作り上げる	to build up	U5	L2	LC2
(いろを)つける	(色を)付ける	to add (color)	U3	L1	LC1
(すみを)つける	(墨を)付ける	to put (ink)	U3	L2	LC1
(さべつに)つながる	(差別に)つながる	to lead to (descrimination)	U6	L2	LC2
つなぐ	つなぐ	to connect	U2	L2	LC1
つらい	つらい	hardship	U4	L2	LC2

て

であい	出会い	encounter	U3	L2	LC2
であう	出会う	to encounter, to meet	U4	L2	LC2
てき	敵	enemy	U4	L1	LC2
でんしメール	電子メール	electronic mail	U1	L1	LC1
でんとうてき	伝統的	traditionally	U3	L2	LC2

と

どうが	動画	video clip	U1	L1	LC1
どうぐ	道具	tool	U3	L2	LC1
とうじ	当時	at that time, then	U4	L1	LC2
とうじょうする	登場する	to appear, make an appearnce	U1	L1	LC1
(~を)とおして	(~を)通して	through ~	U1	L1	LC1
とくいな	得意な	skillful	U6	L1	LC1
どくしょ	読書	reading	U6	L1	LC2
とくせい	特性	characteristics	U5	L1	LC2
とくちょう	特徴	characteristics	U2	L1	LC1
とくべつ	特別	special	U4	L2	LC2
としうえ	年上	older person	U4	L2	LC2
としかいはつ	都市開発	urban development	U2	L2	LC2
とち	土地	land, plot	U4	L1	LC1
(たいせいが)ととのう	(態勢が)整う	to be ready	U5	L1	LC1
(ふでを)ととのえる	(筆を)整える	to adjust (the brush)	U3	L2	LC1
(つうちを)とめる	(通知を)止める	to deactivate (notification)	U1	L2	LC2
(ふでを)とめる	(筆を)止める	to stop (the brush)	U3	L2	LC1
ともに	ともに	along with	U5	L1	LC2
とりくみ	取り組み	attempt, effort	U2	L2	LC1

とりくむ	取り組む	to work on	U6	L2	LC1
どりょく(をする)	努力(をする)	(to make) an effort	U5	L1	LC2
どりょくする	努力する	to make an effort	U6	L2	LC1
(コミュニケーションを)とる	(コミュニケーションを)取る	to have (a communication)	U1	L1	LC1
(しゃしん/どうがを)とる	(写真/動画を)撮る	to take a (picture/video)	U1	L1	LC1
(ちがいを)とわず	(違いを)問わず	regardless of, no matter	U5	L1	LC2

な

ないよう	内容	content	U2	L2	LC1
(いぞんしょうを)なおす	(依存症を)治す	to cure (addiction)	U1	L2	LC2
ながいす	長椅子	long stool	U3	L2	LC2
なかば	半ば	in the middle of	U4	L2	LC1
ながもちする	長持ちする	to last long time, durability	U2	L1	LC2
ながれる	流れる	to flow	U5	L2	LC2
なみ	波	wave	U3	L1	LC1
なやむ	悩む	to have a trouble diciding	U1	L1	LC2
なんてん	難点	cons, disadvantage	U1	L2	LC1
なんとなく	なんとなく	unintentionally	U5	L2	LC1
なんみん	難民	refugee	U4	L2	LC2

に

にじ	虹	rainbow	U5	L2	LC2
(せんが)にじむ	(線が)にじむ	(lines) smear	U3	L2	LC1
にちじょうせいかつ	日常生活	daily life	U2	L2	LC1
にっけい	日系	Japanese heritage	U4	L1	LC1
にどと(〜ない)	二度と(〜ない)	never again	U4	L1	LC1
にんき(がある)	人気(がある)	popular	U1	L1	LC2

ね

ねがい	願い	wish, hope	U6	L2	LC2
ねだん	値段	price, cost	U2	L1	LC2
ねんちょう	年長	the oldest	U4	L2	LC2
ねんねん	年々	year after year	U5	L1	LC1
ねんれい	年齢	age	U2	L1	LC2

の

のう	脳	brain	U1	L2	LC1
のうじょう	農場	farmland	U4	L2	LC2
のうそん	農村	farming village	U4	L1	LC1
のうたん	濃淡	dark/light color contrast	U3	L2	LC1
(せんそうから)のがれる	(戦争から)逃れる	to escape (from war)	U4	L1	LC2
(かぞくを)のこす	(家族を)残す	to leave (family) behind	U4	L2	LC2
のみこむ	飲み込む	to swallow	U3	L1	LC1
のりこえる	乗り越える	to overcome	U6	L1	LC2

は

は	葉	leaf	U3	L2	LC1
ばい	倍	twice, of times	U5	L2	LC1
はいけい	背景	background	U4	L1	LC1
ばいしょうきん	賠償金	financial compensation	U4	L1	LC1
はくがい	迫害	persecution	U4	L2	LC1
はずかしい	恥ずかしい	embarrased	U5	L2	LC2
はち	鉢	bowl	U3	L2	LC2
はってん	発展	development	U6	L2	LC1
はば	幅	width	U3	L2	LC2
はらう	払う	to pay	U4	L1	LC1
はんがえ	版画絵	Woodblock paint	U3	L1	LC1
はんたいする	反対する	to oppose, to against	U4	L1	LC2
はんぶん	半分	half	U5	L2	LC1

ひ

び	美	beauty	U3	L2	LC1
ヒーローもの	ヒーローもの	hero things	U6	L2	LC2
びじゅつかんしょう	美術鑑賞	art appreciation	U3	L1	LC2
ひつようがない	必要がない	unnecessary	U1	L2	LC1
ビデオつうわ(をする)	ビデオ通話(をする)	(to make) a video call	U1	L1	LC2
ひとがら	人柄	personality	U4	L1	LC2
ひとりぐらし	一人暮らし	live alone	U2	L2	LC1
ひょうか	評価	evaluation, rating	U2	L1	LC2
ひょうかされる	評価される	recognized, is valued, praised	U2	L2	LC1
ひょうげんする	表現する	to express	U3	L1	LC2
びようし	美容師	beautician	U4	L2	LC2
ひょうじする	表示する	to display	U2	L2	LC1
びょうどう	平等	equality	U3	L2	LC2
ひょうばん	評判	reputation	U2	L1	LC2
ひろい	広い	wide, vast	U5	L1	LC2
ひんこん	貧困	poverty	U4	L2	LC1
ひんしつ	品質	quality	U2	L1	LC2

ふ

ふうけい	風景	scenery	U3	L1	LC1
ふきゅう	普及	spread, widespread	U1	L1	LC1
ふし	節	joints	U3	L2	LC1
ふっくら	ふっくら	fluffy	U2	L1	LC1
ふっこう	復興	restration, rebuild	U4	L1	LC2
ふで	筆	brush	U3	L2	LC1
ぶぶん	部分	parts	U3	L2	LC1
ふべん	不便	inconvenient	U2	L2	LC2
ふまん	不満	complain	U5	L1	LC2
ふむ	踏む	to stomp	U3	L1	LC1
プラスチックせいひん	プラスチック製品	plastic goods	U6	L2	LC1
(いけんに)ふれる	(意見に)触れる	to encounter (opinion)	U5	L1	LC2
ぶんか	文化	culture	U5	L1	LC1
ぶんぼうぐ	文房具	stationary	U2	L1	LC1

へ

へいわ	平和	peace	U3	L2	LC2
へる	減る	to decrease	U1	L2	LC1
へんけん	偏見	prejudice	U6	L2	LC2

ほ

ほうかご	放課後	after school	U6	L1	LC2
ほうげん	方言	dilect	U4	L1	LC2
ほおん	保温	keep warm	U2	L1	LC1
ほし	星	stars	U3	L1	LC2
ほぞんする	保存する	to store, to keep	U1	L1	LC2
ほほえむ	微笑む	to smile, to grin	U4	L1	LC2

ボランティアかつどう	ボランティア活動	volunteer activity	U6 L1 LC2
ほる	彫る	to carve	U3 L1 LC1

ま

まげる	曲げる	to curb	U3 L2 LC1
まざる	混ざる	blend	U5 L2 LC1
まじめ	まじめ	serious, studious	U5 L1 LC1
まぜる	混ぜる	to mix	U3 L2 LC1
まだまだ	まだまだ	not yet	U6 L2 LC2
まちがう	間違う	to make mistake	U6 L2 LC2
まなぶ	学ぶ	to learn	U5 L1 LC1
(かんきょうを)まもる	(環境を)守る	to protect (the environment)	U6 L2 LC1

み

みかた(になる)	味方(になる)	(to be) on your side	U6 L2 LC2
みき	幹	trunk	U3 L2 LC1
みため	見た目	appearance	U2 L2 LC2
みちあんない	道案内	a guide, directions	U1 L1 LC1
みとめる	認める	to admit	U4 L1 LC1
みなおす	見直す	to reflect	U5 L2 LC1
みぶん	身分	status	U3 L2 LC2

む

むかえる	迎える	to greet	U2 L2 LC1
むかし	昔	past	U1 L1 LC1
むきあう	向き合う	to face	U5 L2 LC2
むちゅう(になる)	夢中(になる)	to be passionate	U6 L1 LC1
むり	無理	impossible	U1 L2 LC2
むりょう	無料	free of charge, no fee	U1 L1 LC2

め

めざす	目指す	to advance	U5 L1 LC2
めざましどけい	目覚まし時計	alarm clock	U1 L2 LC2

も

もくひょう	目標	goal	U6 L2 LC1
もっていく	持って行く	to take (thing) to a place	U1 L2 LC2
もてなす	もてなす	to entertain	U3 L2 LC2
(しごとを)もとめる	(仕事を)求める	to seek for (a job)	U4 L1 LC1
もともと	もともと	originally	U4 L2 LC1
ものごと	物事	things	U6 L1 LC2

や

やがて	やがて	gradually, finally	U4 L2 LC2
やく〜	約〜	about ~, approximately	U3 L2 LC2
やく	役	role	U6 L2 LC2
やくだつ	役立つ	useful	U1 L1 LC2
やくにたつ	役に立つ	to be useful	U6 L1 LC2
(かんきょうに)やさしい	(環境に)優しい	(environmentally) friendly	U2 L2 LC2
やさしさ	優しさ	kindness	U4 L1 LC2
やすらぎ	安らぎ	comfort	U2 L2 LC1
やっと	やっと	finally	U6 L2 LC2
やりがい	やりがい	worth doing	U5 L1 LC2

ゆ

ゆうぐうする	優遇する	to favor	U5 L1 LC2
ゆうしゅうな	優秀な	outstanding	U5 L1 LC2
ゆうりょう	有料	fee, charge	U1 L1 LC2
ゆたか(にする)	豊か(にする)	to enrich	U2 L2 LC1
ゆたかな	豊かな	richness, bountiful	U4 L2 LC1
ゆめみる	夢見る	to dream about	U4 L2 LC1
(けっこんを)ゆるす	(結婚を)許す	to give a permission (for a marriage)	U4 L1 LC2

よ

ようす	様子	condition, state, situation	U1 L1 LC1
よごす	汚す	to make thing dirty	U6 L2 LC1
よぞら	夜空	nightly sky	U3 L1 LC2
よはく	余白	empty space, blank space	U3 L2 LC1
よびかた	呼び方	the way to call	U5 L2 LC1
よゆう(がない)	余裕(がない)	no leeway, tight on money	U2 L2 LC1
よろこび	喜び	joy	U6 L1 LC1
よろこぶ	喜ぶ	to joy, to rejoice	U2 L2 LC1

ら

〜らしい	〜らしい	like ~	U6 L2 LC2

り

りかいしあう	理解し合う	to understand mutually	U6 L2 LC2
りかいする	理解する	to comprehend	U2 L2 LC1
りてん	利点	pro, advantage	U1 L2 LC1
りゆう	理由	reason	U5 L1 LC1
りゅうがくする	留学する	to study abroad	U5 L2 LC2
りゅうがくせい	留学生	exchange student	U5 L1 LC2
りゅうこうする	流行する	to become popular	U3 L1 LC1
りょう	量	amount, quantity	U3 L2 LC1
りよう	利用	usage, use	U1 L1 LC1
りょうしん	両親	parents	U4 L2 LC2
りようする	利用する	to use	U1 L1 LC2

る

ルーツ	ルーツ	root	U5 L2 LC1

れ

れきし	歴史	history	U4 L1 LC1
れんらくする	連絡する	to contact (someone)	U1 L1 LC2

ろ

ろうどうしゃ	労働者	labor	U5 U5 LC2

わ

わかもの	若者	young person, young generation	U1 L1 LC2
(じかんを)わすれる	(時間を)忘れる	to forget (time)	U6 L1 LC1
(うみ/かわを)わたる	(海/川を)渡る	to cross (river/ocean)	U4 L2 LC2
わるぎ(はない)	悪気(はない)	not intentional	U5 L2 LC1

About the Authors

Yo Azama (安座間 喜治)

Lead Instructional Coach at Salinas Union High School District (サリナス学校区 教育指導主任)

Yo Azama is a teacher, learner, presenter, workshop facilitator, author, musician, and husband. He currently serves as the Lead Instructional Coach at Salinas Union High School District where he designs and facilitates professional development for faculty members. Prior to this position he taught Japanese at the elementary, middle, and high school levels for over 20 years and a Teaching Method course at California State University, Monterey Bay for 5 years. He received the prestigious ACTFL National Language Teacher of the Year Award in 2012.

Atsuko Kiuchi-Fagerness (木内 厚子)

Japanese Teacher at Elk Grove High school (エルクグローブ高校 日本語教師)

Atsuko is a teacher, learner, mother, wife, traveler, and animal lover. Born in Tokyo. Atsuko's teaching journey started 23 years ago. She loves having the opportunity to be a part of her students' lives via the exchange of the Japanese language and culture. She is the current president of the California Association of Japanese Language Teachers and also is a leadership team member of the Capital World Language Project. As her curiosity as a teacher and as a human has only grown with age, Atsuko's motto remains "Never stop learning!"

Mio Nishimura (西村 美緒)

Japanese Teacher at Alisal High School (アリサル高校 日本語教師)

Mio is a learner, teacher, mentor teacher, mother, wife, swimmer, karaoke enthusiast, and lover of owarai. Her passion is to learn languages and cultures with students, her inspiration is to work with students, colleagues, and community members, and her favorite quote is from the Buddha: "The mind is everything. What you think, you become." She received an Outstanding Teacher Award from the California Language Teachers Association in 2018. She has also been a boys' volleyball coach and received a Coach of the Year award. Currently, she teaches at Alisal High School, leads the Japanese program for Salinas Union High School District, and is a team leader of the Monterey Bay World Language Project.

Michelle Lupisan (ミシェル ルピサン)

Japanese Teacher at Salinas High School (サリナス高校 日本語教師)

Michelle is a teacher, a learner, an artist, and is passionate about health and wellness. She enjoys partaking in many forms of creativity, such as illustration, theatre, cooking, filmmaking, and poetry. She began studying Japanese in high school, and has lived in Japan for two years both as a student and as an English teacher. Currently, she is in her fifth year of teaching Japanese at Salinas High School, and enjoys making connections with her students through their mutual love for the language and culture.

COMPASS JAPANESE INTERMEDIATE INTERACTIVE WORKBOOK

コンパス日本語　中級

2022年6月11日　第1刷発行

著　　者● 安座間 喜治・木内 厚子・西村 美緒・ミシェル ルピサン
発 行 人● 岡野秀夫
発 行 所● くろしお出版
〒102-0084　東京都千代田区二番町4-3
Tel: 03-6261-2867　Fax: 03-6261-2879
URL: https://www.9640.jp　Email: kurosio@9640.jp
印　　刷● シナノ書籍印刷

編集協力● 株式会社エスクリプト
イラスト● レッスン扉：タカセ マサヒロ
その他：畠中 美幸
本文デザイン● 風間 新吾
装丁デザイン● 鈴木 章宏
音　　声● ボイスプロ

写真・画像

- p.96, p.97 ◎葛飾北斎『冨嶽三十六景 神奈川沖浪裏』『冨嶽三十六景 凱風快晴』『諸国滝廻り 下野黒髪山きりふりの滝』東京国立博物館所蔵 ◎歌川広重『名所江戸百景 大はしあたけの夕立』『東海道五十三次 蒲原夜之雪』『東海道五十三次 日本橋朝之景』『東海道五十三次 庄野白雨』東京国立博物館所蔵 ◎歌川広重『名所江戸百景 逆井のわたし』国立国会図書館所蔵
- p.105, p.106, p.112 ◎フィンセント・ファン・ゴッホ『夜のカフェテラス』『ひまわり』ゴッホ美術館所蔵 ◎ピエール=オーギュスト・ルノワール『ピアノに寄る少女たち』オルセー美術館所蔵 ◎エドヴァルド・ムンク『叫び』オスロ国立美術館所蔵 ◎クロード・モネ『ラ・ジャポネーズ』ボストン美術館所蔵
- p.117 ◎小林東雲「水墨画　竹」https://www.youtube.com/watch?v=aw4kEVDSx9A&t=120s
- p.125 ◎長谷川等伯『千利休像』春屋宗園賛 ◎「つくばい」「にじり口」「茶室の中」写真AC
- p.137 ◎Joseph Dwight Strong『明治拾八年に於ける布哇砂糖耕地の情景』◎「強制収容される日系アメリカ人」U.S. National Archives and Records Administration ◎「日本海軍の攻撃で炎上する戦艦「アリゾナ」」U.S. National Archives and Records Administration ◎「太平洋戦争に於ける日本の降伏文書調印」Naval Historical Center

ISBN978-4-87424-902-4 C0081

Connections to AP Unit Guides and IB Themes

COMPASS INTERACTIVE WORKBOOK provides meaningful learning experiences by investigating rich human experiences through Japanese cultures while promoting language proficiency of the Intermediate (low-mid) level on the ACTFL proficiency scales. This is suitable for learners who are approaching the intermediate level. Below chart shows the alignment between the Compass contents, the AP Unit Guides topics, and IB themes. AP Japanese and IB teachers may find this useful as they design their curriculum and scope and sequence.

Compass Unit Theme & Lesson Topics	AP Unit Guides Topics	IB Themes
Unit 1 **私たちの生活とテクノロジー** **Technology and Our Lives** **L1 ● スマホで生活向上** Improved Life with Smartphones **L2 ● スマホと私** Smartphone and I	How Science and Technology Affect Our Lives (Unit 4)	Identities Human Ingenuity
Unit 2 **進化するデザイン** **Evolving Design** **L1 ● 日本の製品とデザイン** Japanese Products and Design **L2 ● いいデザインの要素** Elements of Good Design	Factors That Impact the Quality of Life (Unit 5)	Identities Human Ingenuity
Unit 3 **日本芸術への響き** **Be Inspired by Japanese Art** **L1 ● 美術の楽しみ方** How to Enjoy Art **L2 ● 文化体験** Cultural Experience	Influence of Beauty and Art (Unit 3)	Identities Human Ingenuity